CRACKLE WEAVE
SIMPLY

CRACKLE WEAVE
SIMPLY

UNDERSTANDING THE WEAVE STRUCTURE

27 PROJECTS TO PRACTICE YOUR SKILLS

SUSAN KESLER-SIMPSON

STACKPOLE BOOKS

Essex, Connecticut
Blue Ridge Summit, Pennsylvania

STACKPOLE BOOKS

An imprint of Globe Pequot, the trade division of
The Rowman & Littlefield Publishing Group, Inc.
4501 Forbes Blvd., Ste. 200
Lanham, MD 20706
www.rowman.com

Distributed by NATIONAL BOOK NETWORK
800-462-6420

British Library Cataloguing in Publication Information
available

Library of Congress Cataloging-in-Publication Data

Names: Kesler-Simpson, Susan, author.
Title: Crackle weave simply / Susan Kesler-Simpson.
Description: First edition. | Lanham, MD : Stackpole Books, an
    imprint of Globe Pequot, the trade division of The Rowman
    & Littlefield Publishing Group, Inc., 2022. | Includes
    bibliographical references and index. | Summary: "The
    areas of separating threads give crackle weave its appearance
    of cracking pottery, and once you see how the structure
    works, there is so much you can do with it! Learning is not
    complete without practice, so there are numerous patterns to
    try for a variety of pieces and both modern and traditional
    effects"— Provided by publisher.
Identifiers: LCCN 2021050396 (print) | LCCN 2021050397
    (ebook) | ISBN 9780811769983 (paperback ; permanent
    paper) | ISBN 9780811769990 (epub)
Subjects: LCSH: Hand weaving—Patterns. | Crackle weave.
Classification: LCC TT848 .K373 2022 (print) | LCC TT848
    (ebook) | DDC 746.1/4—dc23/eng/20211209
LC record available at https://lccn.loc.gov/2021050396
LC ebook record available at https://lccn.loc.gov/2021050397

First Edition

CONTENTS

CHAPTER 1

What Is So Special about Crackle Weave?

Crackle weave is Swedish in origin. It is a beautiful weave structure that sadly has often been overlooked in the weaving community. In our quest to learn or do something current and exciting, we often forget how beautiful and adaptable the traditional weave structures can be.

The name comes from the crackling that happens to the glaze on some pottery when it is fired. The glaze separates and allows the color underneath to emerge. Figure 1.1 shows the "crackle" in this weave structure.

Figure 1.1. Close-up of crackle weave, showing the "crackle."

Crackle weave has generally been associated with upholstery fabrics and considered inappropriate for wearing apparel. But with the new fibers that we now have available, we can use this weave structure in many different ways. The projects in this book include shawls, table runners, scarves, and a rug.

Crackle weave is one of those weave structures that can easily be modified to fit in a modern setting or woven to fit into a traditional setting. This cannot be said about all of the other weave structures. When

you see overshot or shadow weave, you automatically think traditional. And making these weave structures fit a modern setting can be challenging.

With crackle weave, you design with blocks. The pattern block is created by the floats of the larger weft thread, much the same as overshot. This thread is not as visible in the background blocks. The blocks can be enlarged or reduced, and/or you can change their location to create new designs. You can weave a project with a more traditional look or change the block size and location and make the piece more modern.

And then there is color! Crackle weave offers many options because of this block structure. Colors can be added through the warp, primary threads, and/or secondary/tabby threads. Doing something as simple as alternating two colors of the secondary thread can add a wonderful new design element.

My goal through this book is to give you a basic understanding of crackle weave on which you can expand. I will explain crackle weave in a simple, straightforward manner that is easy to understand. I've included numerous projects that will let you try out your new skills. These projects are not difficult and will give you the basic skills on which to build. The more experienced weaver will easily be able to adapt these patterns to their level of expertise. Most of the projects are for 4-shaft looms, since this is the most common type that weavers use. This is not intended to be an in-depth study of crackle weave. If you fall in love with crackle and wish to learn more, there are books available with additional information. Susan Wilson's *Weave Classic Crackle and More* is a fantastic book with incredible detail. Once you learn and understand the basics of the structure, there are no limits to what you can create.

CHAPTER 2

Understanding Crackle Weave: Four-Shaft Loom

Crackle weave is a 4-thread point twill weave structure. The odd/even rule that is followed in twill has to be followed in crackle weave. Keep this rule in mind as we learn about this weave structure. Crackle weave has a pattern thread and a secondary thread. The secondary thread is generally half the size of the pattern thread.

Threading

Crackle weave is a block weave. Each of these blocks is made up of 4 threads in a 4-point twill fashion. Figure 2.1 shows the blocks for 4 shafts. **Regardless of the tie-up for your projects, the composition of these blocks does not change.**

Next let's look at putting these blocks together. Begin by looking at Block A and Block B. If you were to try to put these two blocks next to each other, you would have two "2"s in a row. Following the odd/even threading of twill would mean that this is incorrect. So

we will need to add an *incidental thread*. An incidental thread is one that is added to complete a block and maintain the odd/even threading pattern. In crackle weave it is very simple! The incidental thread will always be the *same as the first thread in that block*. So the incidental thread for the A Block would be a 1. The incidental thread for the B Block will be 2, and so on. In Figure 2.2, you will see the same blocks but with the incidental threads added and highlighted in green.

NOTE: In the projects, the incidental thread is still indicated by a green block. However, instead of the shaft number, you will see an X.

You can repeat any of the blocks multiple times before you need to add an incidental. The incidental is only added when moving from one block to the next, as shown in Figure 2.3. This chart shows two Blocks A, one Block B, two Blocks C, and two Blocks D. The blocks have been outlined in bold so that you can easily see the breakdown.

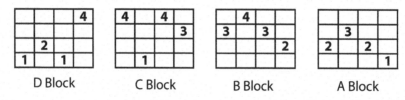

Figure 2.1. The blocks for 4-point twill.

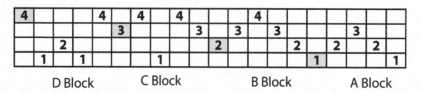

Figure 2.2. Incidental threads are added and highlighted in green.

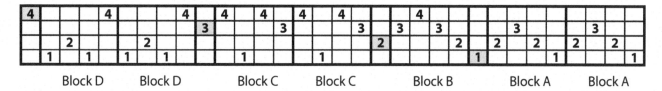

Block D   Block D   Block C   Block C   Block B   Block A   Block A

Figure 2.3. You can repeat blocks multiple times, adding the incidental thread only when moving from one block to the next.

But what if I want to go from Block A to Block C? Can I do that? Absolutely! This is how it would work. Figure 2.4 shows the two blocks.

If you look at combining the blocks, you can see that you would have a "2" thread followed by a "3" thread. That would work! But to get a better overall balance and appearance, it is best to add two incidental threads. This step would complete Block A before moving to Block C, as shown in Figure 2.5.

Here you will see that two incidental threads have been added and are highlighted in green. The "1" thread completes the A Block, and the "2" thread maintains the odd/even rule.

Follow the same procedure when working with 8 shafts. When combining blocks in this manner, you will get a break in the design. The Highlands Table Runner (page 111) is one of the projects that demonstrates this technique. This runner is an 8-shaft piece. The sequence in the threading is A, B, C, D. The next blocks are H, G, F, and E. You can see a definite break between D and H, and also E and A. In each case you will see the use of two incidental threads. It creates a

very interesting design! Just so you know, the more shafts you have, the greater this effect will be.

But let's think outside the box when planning your threading. How about adding a rose path twill threading in between some of the crackle weave blocks! Since this structure is based on twills, this is a perfect way to accent the blocks and give more interest to your piece. If you look at the Blocks of Thyme Shawl (page 47), you will see that a straight twill threading has been inserted in the threading draft. This gives an outline to the lacy crackle weave blocks, as well as more overall stability. Just remember that if you do this, be sure to follow the odd/even rule, adding incidental threads as needed.

Treadling

Next we need to look at treadling crackle weave. The same block construction occurs in the treadling as in the threading. Figure 2.6 shows the four blocks.

You can easily see the similarity with the threading blocks. And once again, since we are working with a twill, the odd/even rule must be maintained when

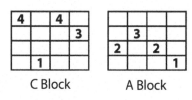

C Block   A Block

Figure 2.4. Block A and Block C.

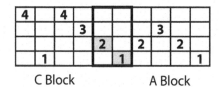

C Block   A Block

Figure 2.5. Block A and C with incidental threads added.

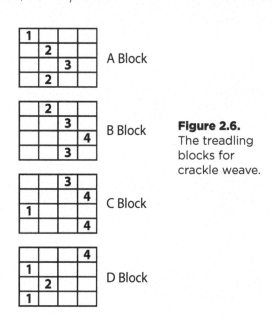

Figure 2.6. The treadling blocks for crackle weave.

A Block

B Block

C Block

D Block

moving from Block A to Block B. Figure 2.7 shows the addition of the incidental thread highlighted in green.

It is important to note that when treadling you will be working with a pattern thread and a secondary thread. In the treadling pattern blocks where the number is repeated, that will be where you will be using the pattern thread. Another way that you will see this indicated in the projects is shown in Figure 2.7.

Just as in the threading sequence, the incidental thread is always the same thread as the first thread in that block. So for Block A, the incidental thread is "1," for Block B the incidental thread is "2," and so on (see Figure 2.8).

NOTE: In the projects the incidental thread is still indicated by a green block. However, instead of the shaft number, you will see an X.

You can easily treadle Block A and then Block C by adding two incidental threads, just as you did in the threading. Figure 2.9 shows this combination. The incidental threads are highlighted in green.

And just as in the threading, since we are working with a twill structure, it is easy to add a different twill pattern. Looking again at the Blocks of Thyme Shawl (page 47) you will see a straight twill intermixed with the crackle treadling. Just be sure that if you do this, you follow the odd/even rule. Add incidental threads as needed.

Tie-Up for 4-Shaft Crackle

The tie-up for 4-shaft crackle is a balanced tie-up, so we are looking at the traditional 2/2 twill tie-up (Figure 2.10).

All of the 4-shaft projects in this book use this tie-up. However, you will find crackle weave tie-ups that are 2/2 twill but arranged differently. How does this affect the pattern? Does it make any difference? The answer is YES! What will change is the location of the blocks. In Figures 2.11–2.14, you will see that the tie-up has changed. So you need to look at the position of the blocks within the design. This is where a computer program comes in handy, as it allows you to quickly see whether you want to start with a different block in your treadling.

In Figure 2.11 you can see that there are 3 dark sections in the upper left corner. In Figure 2.12, the tie-up is still a 2/2 tie-up but positioned differently. The upper left corner only has one dark section now. In

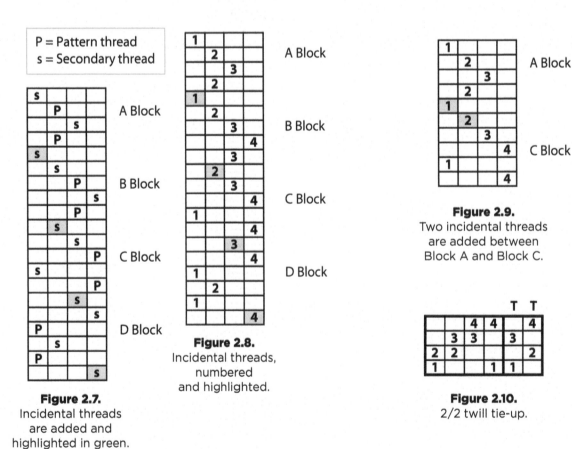

P = Pattern thread
s = Secondary thread

Figure 2.7.
Incidental threads are added and highlighted in green.

Figure 2.8.
Incidental threads, numbered and highlighted.

Figure 2.9.
Two incidental threads are added between Block A and Block C.

Figure 2.10.
2/2 twill tie-up.

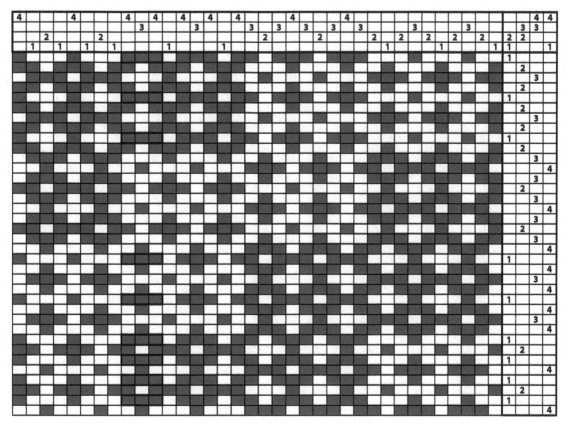

Figure 2.11. In this graph you can see that there are three dark sections in the upper left corner.

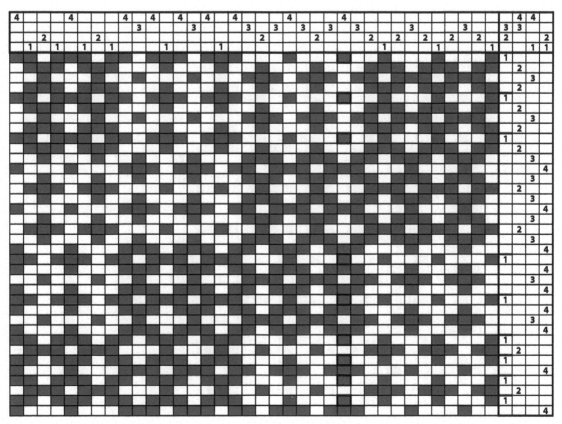

Figure 2.12. The tie-up is still a 2/2 tie-up but positioned differently. The upper left corner only has one dark section now.

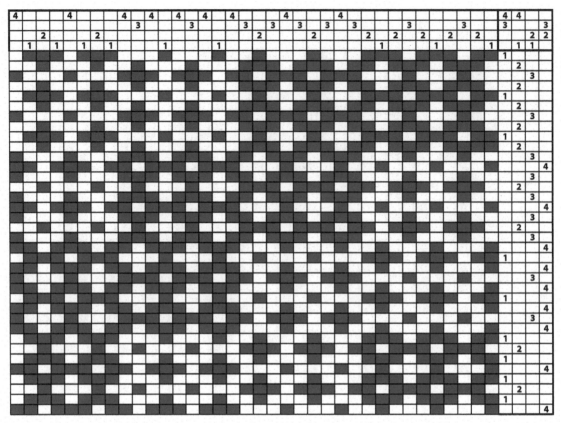

Figure 2.13. The upper left corner is now composed of three light sections.

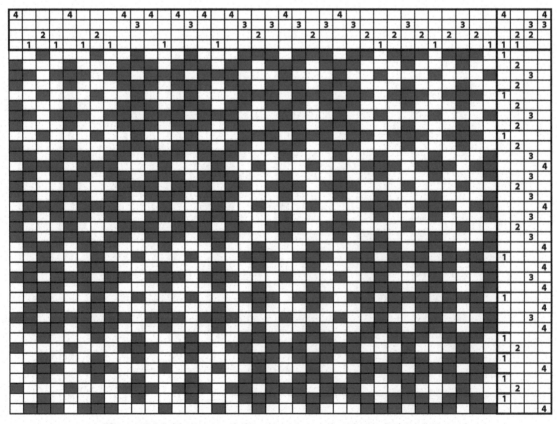

Figure 2.14. The upper left corner is made of one light section.

Figure 2.13, again the tie-up is positioned differently. The upper left corner is now composed of three light sections. And finally, in Figure 2.14, the upper left corner is made of one light section. Study these graphs to see how the position of the blocks changes.

Let's briefly return to the draft in Figure 2.11. One of the wonderful traits of crackle weave is that when weaving it as classic crackle, you will never have a float longer than three threads, so when you are choosing the fiber you want to work with, you can quickly determine how large the floats are going to be. For 10/2 cotton at 24 epi, the float is 0.125 inches, or ⅛ inch. That's a very tiny float. But say you want to weave with wool that is 8 epi. Here the float would be approximately ⅓ inch. This is still a very small float and definitely not a problem in a project, depending on the use of the project—for a baby blanket, that size float may be too long, but it would be just fine for many other uses. In Figure 2.15, I have circled some of the floats. The colored blocks show the float on the right side and the blank blocks would indicate the floats on the reverse.

Substituting Letters in the Threading Draft

If you have looked at the projects in the book, you will see that instead of the threading and treadling being written out in full, letters have been substituted. This is where things can get a bit confusing for some weavers. This is a form of shorthand in weaving. Do not confuse this with profile drafts. Profile drafts only apply if you are working with a unit weave. Crackle weave is not a unit weave, as the blocks share a pattern thread. However, it is a very similar idea.

Let's look again at the threading blocks (see Figure 2.16).

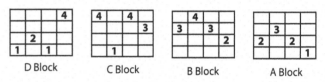

Figure 2.16.
Threading blocks.

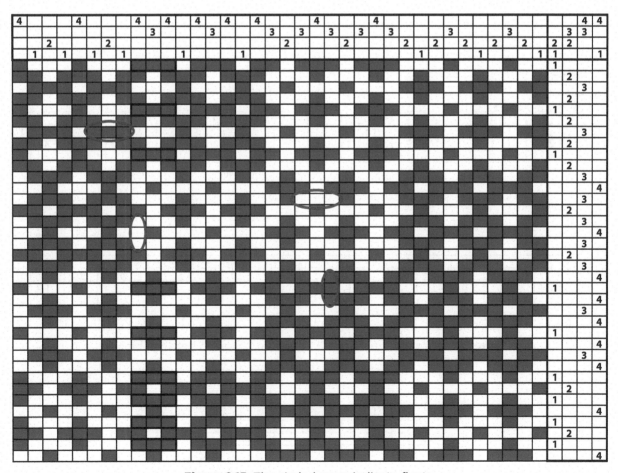

Figure 2.15. The circled areas indicate floats.

Each block has been assigned a letter. In Figure 2.17, you see *letters*, not numbers. Don't overthink this. It is really very simple! The threading for Block A shown in Figure 2.16 is substituted for the A in Figure 2.17. Threading for Block B is substituted for the B, and so on.

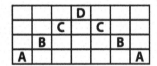

Figure 2.17. Letters are substituted for numbers in the threading.

Figure 2.18 has the numbered blocks substituted for the lettered blocks and shows the threading written in full—*almost!* Can you see what is missing? The incidentals need to be in place. Once again I have inserted them and highlighted them in green (Figure 2.19).

So that there is no confusion for the weaver, the **threading drafts throughout this book will include the incidental threads even where the threading is composed of letters**. Figure 2.20 shows an example.

The charts in Figures 2.19 and 2.20 say the exact same thing, but being able to substitute one letter for four threads dramatically reduces the size of the threading draft. Once you get used to reading a threading draft like this, you will find it very easy to use. If you run into difficulty, it is easy to write out the draft in full and use that instead.

Substituting Letters in the Treadling Draft

The principle is identical for treadling! Again, let's look at the four treadling blocks (see Figure 2.21). You can see that each block has been assigned a letter.

In Figure 2.22, you see letters instead of numbers.

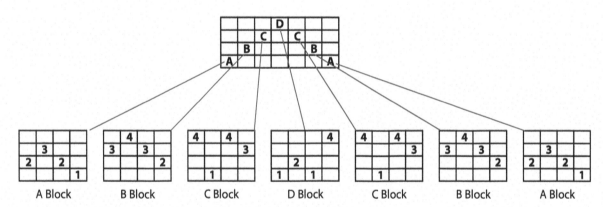

Figure 2.18. Letters are substituted for numbers and the threading is almost complete.

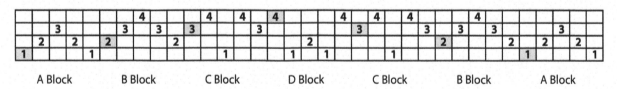

Figure 2.19. Incidentals added and highlighted in green between blocks.

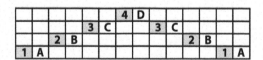

Figure 2.20. Draft with threading blocks represented by letters with numbered incidentals between.

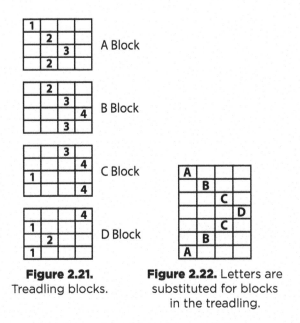

Figure 2.21. Treadling blocks.

Figure 2.22. Letters are substituted for blocks in the treadling.

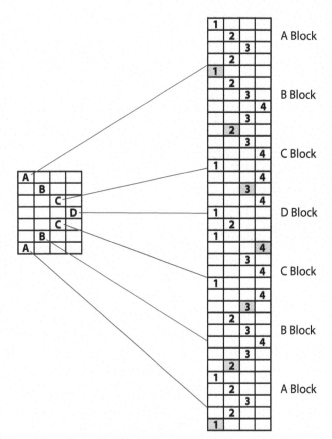

Figure 2.24. Incidentals added and highlighted in green.

Figure 2.23 shows the substitutions, and the treadling draft is written out in full—*almost!*

Once again, we are missing the incidentals! In Figure 2.24, they are added and highlighted in green.

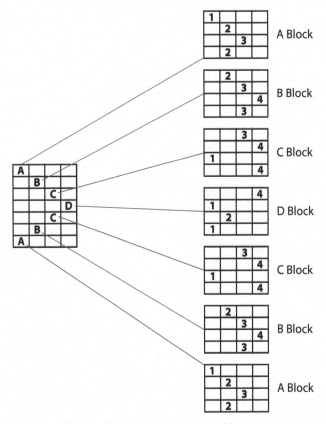

Figure 2.23. Substitutions of letters for numbers is shown.

So that there is no confusion for the weaver, the treadling drafts throughout this book will include the incidental threads even where the threading is composed of letters. Figure 2.25 shows an example of how the treadling drafts will look.

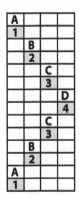

Figure 2.25. Sample treadling showing numbered blocks and highlighted incidental threads.

The charts in Figures 2.24 and 2.25 mean the same thing, just in a different format. Substituting one letter for four threads reduces the length of the treadling charts. Once you get used to using this format, you will find that it is very easy to use.

CHAPTER 3

Understanding Crackle Weave: Eight-Shaft Loom

Adding more shafts to crackle weave opens up many more design options. You will have more blocks to play with, to move around and create the design you want. The pattern block and the background block will still be seen. But a new element is introduced. Now you will be seeing blocks of *plain, or almost plain, weave.* While this adds a new element to the design process, it also presents a problem. As you know, plain weave is a very solid structure, and now you will be placing plain weave next to a pattern block. The problem arises in that the pattern block has the floats. So when you weave your fabric, the plain weave block maintains its structure, but the pattern blocks begin to undulate because the floats are not

structured, and they begin to compress. You can see both the plain weave blocks and the undulation in Figure 3.1. In my sampling, I found that the alternative treadling patterns that included a true tabby were the best to prevent this undulation.

The more repeats of any block, the more undulation you will see. The Shadows Table Runner (page 117) has multiple repeats of blocks as part of the design. When I began weaving this piece, I realized that I needed to use an alternative treadling sequence to maintain the overall structure. The undulation was quite severe. Keep this in mind when designing with more than 4 shafts. And always be open to changing how you will treadle so that your piece looks just as you want.

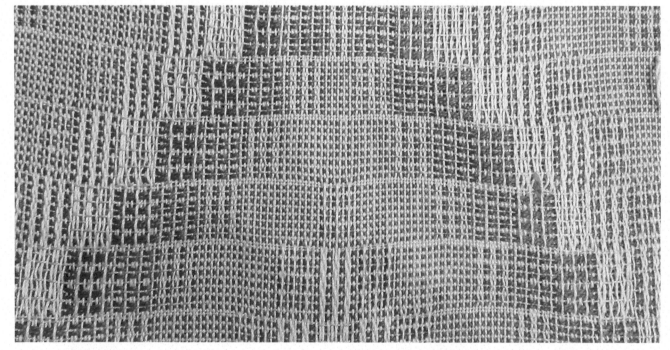

Figure 3.1. Plain weave blocks next to pattern blocks can create undulation in the pattern blocks.

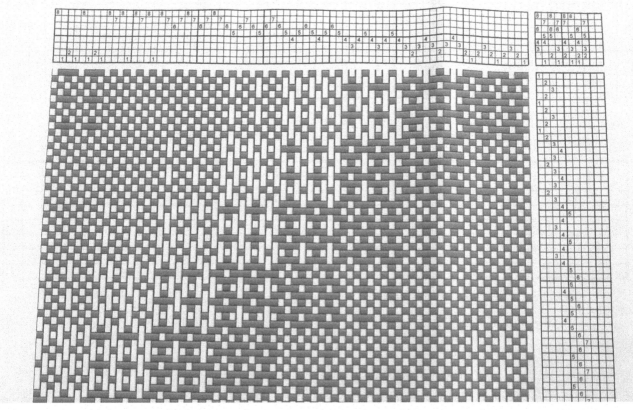

Figure 3.2. Even with 8 shafts, the floats are still 3 threads long.

In the 4-shaft crackle, you learned that all floats are no longer than three threads. This is also true when adding more shafts. Look closely at the graph in Figure 3.2. The floats are still 3 threads long!

Remember that crackle weave is a 4-thread point twill weave structure. The odd/even rule that is followed in twill has to be followed in crackle weave. Crackle weave has a pattern thread and a secondary thread. The secondary thread is generally half the size of the pattern thread. But now we are going to be working with 8 shafts instead of 4. The transition is very easy.

Threading

In 8-shaft crackle, we will have eight separate blocks. These are shown in Figure 3.3. Notice how the individual blocks are arranged. The patterning continues in a systematic and logical fashion, each block building on the last block. The composition of these blocks does not change. If you have a loom with more than 8 shafts, the sequencing would continue in the same manner.

Now we need to look at putting these blocks together. If we were to put the A block next to the B Block, we would have two "2"s together. So once again we will have to add the *incidental* thread. An incidental thread is one that is added to complete a block and maintain the odd/even threading pattern. In crackle weave, the incidental thread is always the same thread as the first thread in that block. So, for Block A, the incidental thread is a "1." For Block B, the incidental thread is a "2," and so on. Figure 3.4 shows the

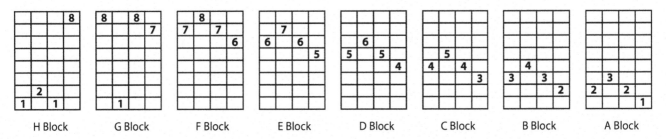

Figure 3.3. Threading blocks for 8-shaft crackle weave.

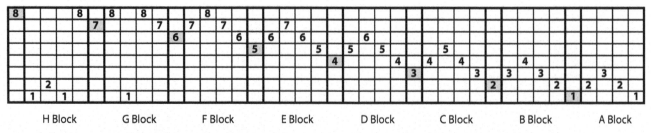

Figure 3.4. Threading with incidental threads added between blocks.

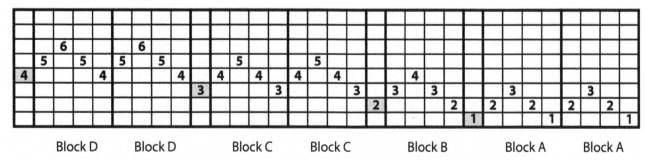

Figure 3.5. Incidental threads are only needed when one block changes to the next one; they are not needed between multiple repeats of the same block.

incidental threads for each block highlighted in green. Adding the incidental thread allows the threading to move from block to block and still maintain the odd/even rule.

The incidental thread is not needed until the block changes. Block A can be repeated as many times as wanted without an incidental thread. Figure 3.5 shows an abbreviated version of a threading that shows repeated blocks and how the incidental thread is used. It is easy to see that there is no need for the incidental thread when the same block is repeated.

NOTE: In the projects the incidental thread is still indicated by a green block. However, instead of the shaft number, you will see an X.

But the question arises: Can I move from the D Block to the H Block or any other configuration? Absolutely! Let's look at these two blocks (Figure 3.6).

To combine these blocks, we have some options. You can see that the D Block ends with an odd number. The H Block begins with an even number 8. Do you have to add an incidental since the odd/even rule is in place? No, you do not, but I like the transition if the incidental threads are added. In our first example (Figure 3.7), we will add two incidental threads. The first incidental is the "4" thread, which balances the D Block. When the "4" thread is added, it *does* become necessary to add another incidental thread. How important is the choice of the second incidental thread? In my experience, I have found that this choice is not significant. You could

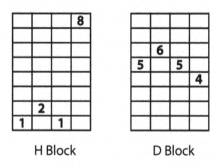

H Block   D Block

Figure 3.6. Blocks D and H.

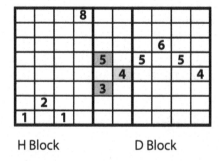

H Block   D Block

Figure 3.7. A "4" incidental thread balances the D Block; the choice for the second incidental is a "3" or "5."

follow a twill pattern, or you could choose one of the threads from the block that you are connecting to. The important thing is to keep the odd/even in place. For the second incidental, you could choose *either* the 5 thread or the 3 thread. These are indicated in pink. This will keep the odd/even rule intact.

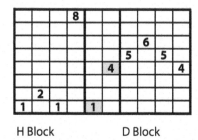

H Block   D Block

Figure 3.8. Here a "1" thread is used as the second incidental.

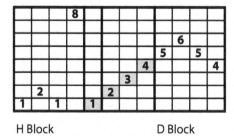

H Block   D Block

Figure 3.9. Here four incidental threads are added between the blocks.

Figure 3.8 shows incidentals connecting the two blocks, but now the second incidental thread is one that is also used in the H Block. In this example, the "1" thread is added, since it is a component of the H Block. The odd/even rule is still intact.

And there is always the next option. In Figure 3.9, four threads have been added to connect the blocks and keep the odd/even rule intact. This method will have the most effect on the overall design.

All of these combinations will work and still maintain the odd/even rule. Your choice may depend on the size of threads that you are using. Smaller threads will have a decreased impact on the overall design, whereas larger threads will be more obvious. To make sure you will be satisfied with your project, it is always a good idea to put the draft into a computer program and make your final decision.

The Highlands Table Runner (page 111) demonstrates the effect that varying the location of the blocks has on the finished piece. Play with the location of the blocks, move them, and rearrange them until you get the look you want. Just keep the odd/even rule in place, and it will work.

Another addition to the threading draft that can be used is to insert a twill design. In the Finale Cape (page 107), point twills were added. If you look closely at the threading draft, you will see that the number of threads added throughout were different. In this design,

the twill threading is used to complete the twill run from block to block. If the crackle block ended with a "5" thread, I chose to do the "4, 3, 2, 1" run and then start the point twill. When the crackle block ended with a "1" thread, I had options again. I chose to do a twill run from "8" to "1," and then I added two more 8-point twill repeats. This was absolutely a choice. You should also note that the number of diamonds changed throughout the piece. But doesn't that make it interesting? Play with the options and create your own designs!

Treadling

Now let's look at the treadling for 8-shaft crackle weave (Figure 3.10). Once again these blocks look very much like the blocks used in the threading.

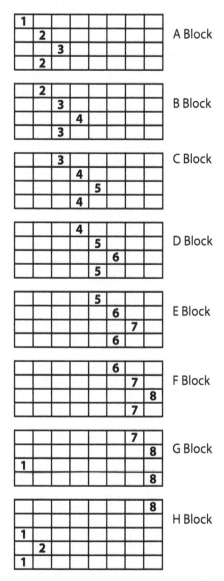

Figure 3.10. Treadling blocks for 8-shaft crackle weave.

Remembering that we are working with a twill sequence and the odd/even rule must be in place, you can see that in order to move from block to block, an incidental thread must be added. The chart in Figure 3.11 shows those incidental threads highlighted in green.

Just as in the threading sequence, the incidental thread is always the same thread as the first thread in that block. So for Block A, the incidental thread is "1," for Block B the incidental thread is "2," and continuing to the H Block the incidental thread would be the "8."

NOTE: In the projects the incidental thread is still indicated by a green block. However, instead of the shaft number, you will see an X.

Just as in the 4-shaft treadling, you are working with a pattern thread and a secondary thread. The repeated number in each block is where you will be using the pattern thread. So if you look at Block A, you can see that the "2" is repeated. That will be your pattern thread. Another way that you will see this indicated in the projects is shown in Figure 3.12.

For design purposes, you might want to skip blocks and move from Block A to Block E. Once again you will need to add incidental threads. But you have options on how to do this.

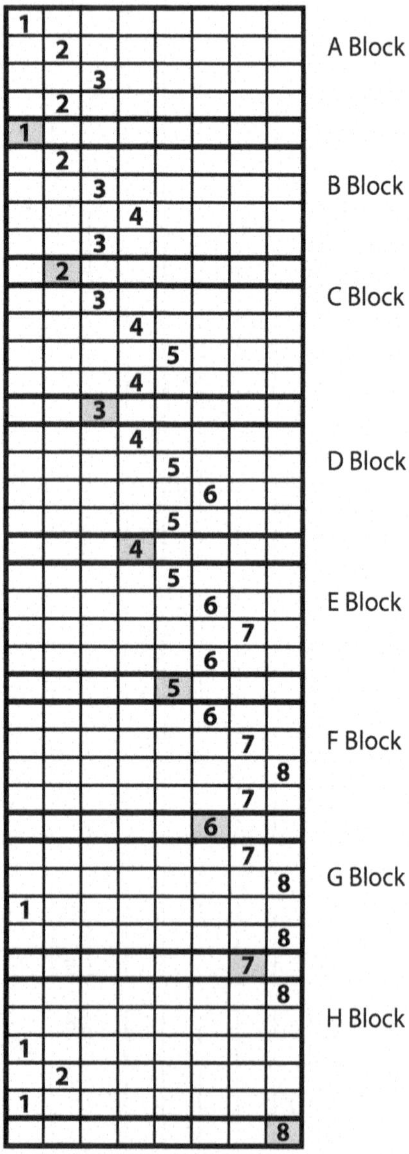

Figure 3.11.
Treadling blocks with incidental threads added.

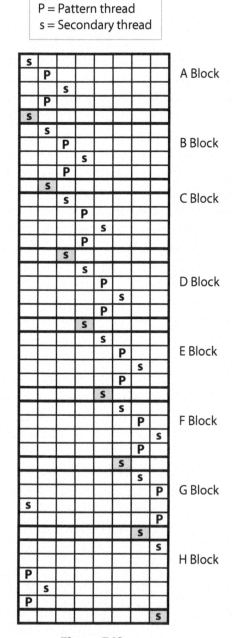

P = Pattern thread
s = Secondary thread

Figure 3.12.
Pattern threads and secondary threads are indicated in the chart.

Since Block A ends with a "2" and Block E starts with a "5," an incidental thread would not be absolutely necessary. You can see this in Figure 3.13.

I, however, like to finish the blocks with the incidental, as in Figure 3.14. In this scenario I have finished Block A with the incidental "1." That necessitates adding a second incidental thread to keep the odd/even rule in place. It does not make any difference what shaft the thread is on. Generally, you will be working with finer threads and the change in the appearance is negligible. If you are unsure, put the draft into a computer weaving program and let that help you decide.

One more option is to add multiple incidental threads, as shown in Figure 3.15. This is essentially

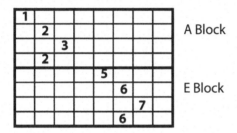

Figure 3.13. When moving from Block A to Block E, an incidental thread is not absolutely necessary.

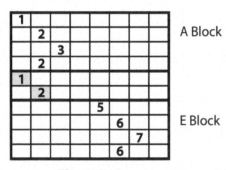

Figure 3.14. Incidental threads added to finish Block A.

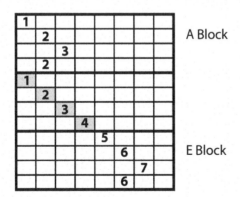

Figure 3.15. Multiple incidental threads added between blocks.

adding a twill to your design. Here you can see that four incidental threads have been added. Adding this many threads will have a larger impact on your design.

These twill additions can become an important part of your design. In the Finale Cape (page 107), you can see that point twills were added in both the threading and the treadling. Adding these twill threadings gave more definition to the crackle blocks as well as introducing the attractive diamonds into the overall design. Just be sure to remember to follow the odd/even rule at all times.

Tie-Up

In this book I used only one tie-up for all of the 8-shaft patterns (Figure 3.16).

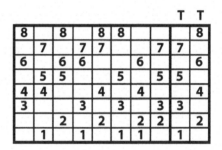

Figure 3.16. Tie-up for 8-shaft crackle weave.

The tie-up was easier to understand when dealing with 4 shafts—not so easy when moving on to 8 shafts. Because the purpose of this book is to simplify and not confuse, I do not want to dwell too much on this material. There are additional tie-ups that can be used, and they will make a difference in the appearance of your finished piece. In the book *Weave Classic Crackle and More* by Susan Wilson, you will find a very extensive write-up regarding the 8-shaft tie-ups. If you wish to delve more fully into this topic, I highly recommend her book. Ultimately what changes is the location of the various blocks.

Substituting Letters in the Threading Draft

When you look at the projects in this book, you will see letters instead of numbers in the threading draft. Let's see how this process works. Figure 3.17 shows the threading blocks written out in full. You can see that each block has been assigned a corresponding letter.

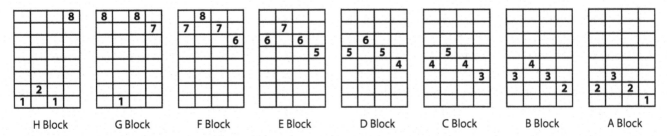

Figure 3.17. Threading blocks for crackle weave.

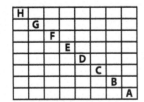

Figure 3.18.
Threading with letters substituted for the blocks.

In Figure 3.18, you will see only letters—no numbers! Don't make this hard! When you see an "A" in the threading, you will substitute all four threads that are a part of Block A. Continue the substitution for each Block A through H.

Figure 3.19 shows the numbered blocks as they relate to the lettered blocks. This threading is complete—*almost!*

Can you see what is missing in this chart? It is the incidental threads. In Figure 3.20, I have inserted the incidental threads and highlighted them in green.

So when you look at the charts in the book you will see them with the letters but also with the highlighted incidental thread. You can see an example in Figure 3.21.

Figures 3.20 and 3.21 mean the exact same thing, but being able to substitute one letter for four threads

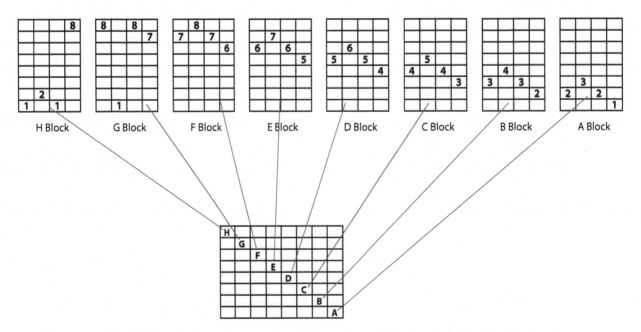

Figure 3.19. Here you can see how the numbered blocks relate to the letters.

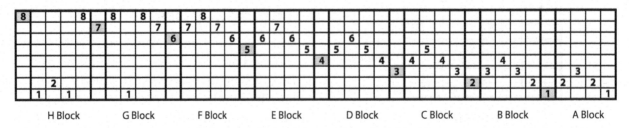

Figure 3.20. Incidental threads added.

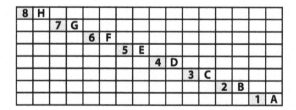

Figure 3.21. Threading showing lettered blocks and highlighted incidental threads.

Substituting Letters in the Treadling Draft

Next we will look at substituting letters for numbers in the treadling drafts. Let's look again at the eight treadling blocks (Figure 3.22). You can see that each block is also assigned a letter.

In Figure 3.23, you see only letters—no numbers!

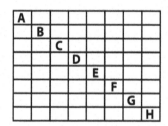

Figure 3.23.
Letters for the blocks are now in the draft.

dramatically reduces the size of the threading draft. Once you get used to reading a threading draft like this, you will find it very easy to use. If you run into problems, it is easy to write out the draft in full and use that instead.

Figure 3.24 shows how the letters correspond to the numbers. This treadling chart is *almost* complete.

A Block

B Block

C Block

D Block

E Block

F Block

G Block

H Block

Figure 3.22.
Treadling blocks for crackle weave.

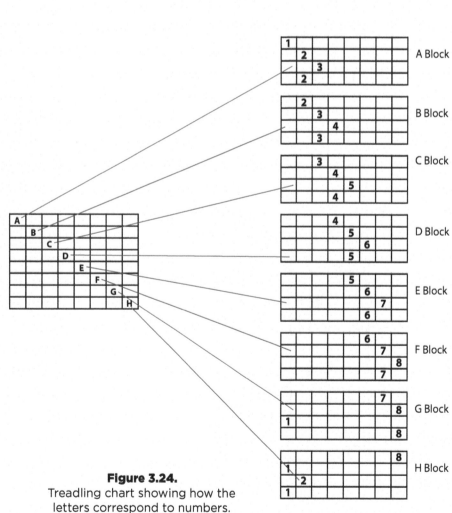

Figure 3.24.
Treadling chart showing how the letters correspond to numbers.

Can you see what is missing? It is the incidental threads. I've added these into the chart in Figure 3.25, highlighted in green.

So that there is no confusion for the weaver, the treadling drafts throughout this book include the incidental threads even where the treadling is composed of letters. An example is shown in Figure 3.26.

The charts in Figures 3.25 and 3.26 mean the same thing, just in a different format. Substituting a letter for four threads reduces the length of the treadling charts. Once you get used to using this format, you will find that it is very easy!

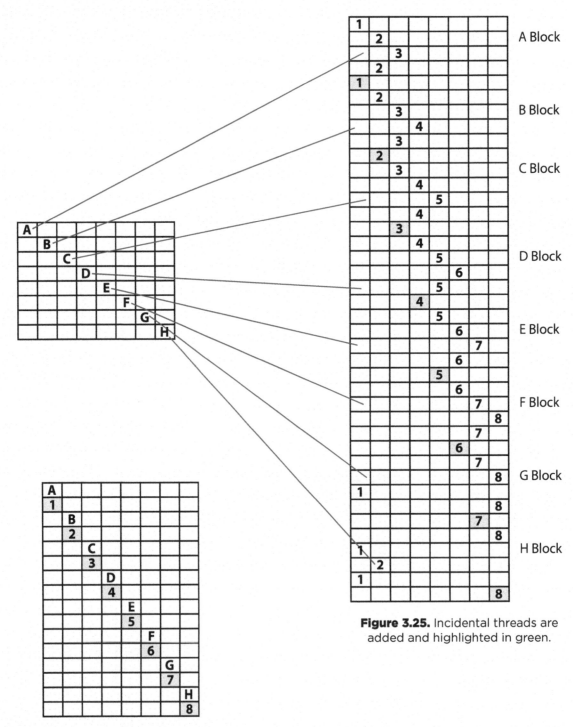

Figure 3.25. Incidental threads are added and highlighted in green.

Figure 3.26. Treadling draft showing letters for blocks and incidental threads highlighted.

CHAPTER 4

Alternative Treadlings for Crackle Weave

For many weavers, getting the loom dressed is quite the process. We want to make all that work worth it, right? We put on a long warp that will be enough for two or more projects, and then what? We've woven the first project and would like to do something different for the next one(s). That is not a problem! In the following sections, we will learn different methods of treadling that we can combine with the crackle threading.

Some of these treadling patterns will result in a distinctly different look. In others, you will see similarities. As you look at these different treadling patterns, think about also changing the number of repeats or the sequence of the blocks. Each small change will give your second or third piece a new look.

This is also a perfect opportunity to change your primary color. Add one or more colors through the secondary thread. Use a textured thread such as a bouclé for the primary thread and see how that looks. This is the time to get creative!

Treadling Italian Manner

Weaving in Italian manner still uses a pattern thread and a secondary thread. The pattern thread is twice the size of the secondary thread. The secondary thread can be the same as the warp thread, or you can use this as an opportunity to introduce another color into your piece.

The way I always think of this technique is "one up–one down." Let's begin by looking at the graph in Figure 4.1. The tie-up is included so you can easily see what shafts will be raised with each treadle.

Let's look closely at the A Block. The pattern thread is on treadle 1. "Move up"—you will depress treadle 2. Then back to treadle 1. "Move down"—you will

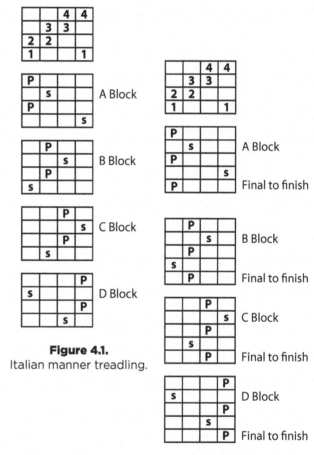

Figure 4.1.
Italian manner treadling.

Figure 4.2.
Final pattern thread added.

depress treadle 4. This completes Block A. All of the blocks work in this fashion. Moving from Block A to Block B is a smooth transition.

There is another way to create this block. This method has three pattern threads in each block since you will end the block with a pattern thread. Figure 4.2 shows the chart with final pattern thread.

If you decide to use this method, you will quickly discover that when moving from block to block you will have two pattern threads next to each other without a secondary thread between them, as indicated in the graph in Figure 4.3. In this graph, the A Block is followed by the B Block.

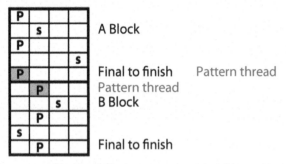

Figure 4.3. Two pattern threads are next to each other.

Eight-shaft patterns follow the same sequence. Figure 4.4 shows the blocks *without* the final pattern thread.

If you add the final pattern thread, once again you will have two pattern threads in a row. Figure 4.5 shows the addition of the final pattern thread.

The obvious question is: Does the addition of the final pattern thread make a difference? I have woven Italian manner both ways. I have not noticed any huge difference. The resulting fabric will still have a wonderful drape.

IMPORTANT NOTE: Because you are not using a true tabby in the 8-shaft Italian manner treadling, you will see more undulation in the blocks. You will have to decide whether you like the results.

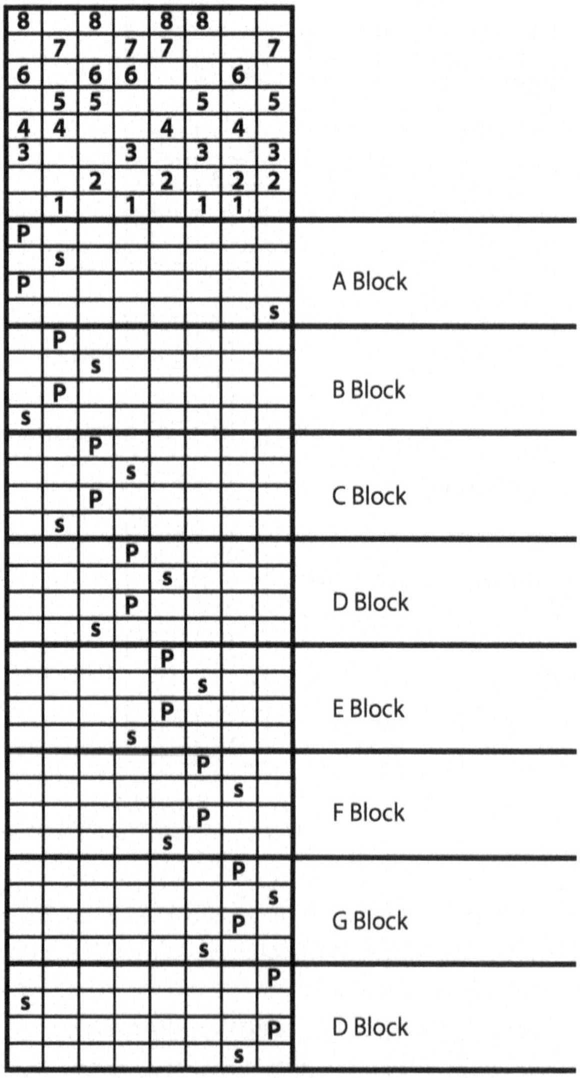

Figure 4.4. Eight-shaft blocks without the final pattern thread.

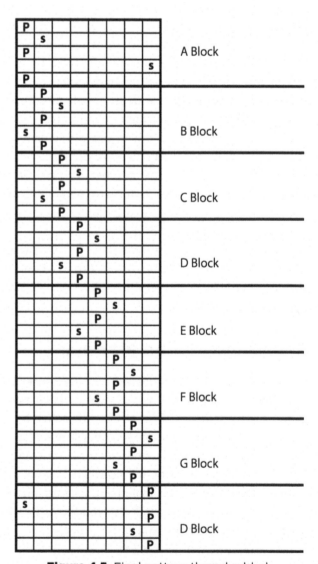

Figure 4.5. Final pattern thread added.

Treadling as Lace

Treadling a crackle threading as lace is easy and a wonderful option when you have a long warp. All of the treadling options are loosely based on actual lace treadling patterns. If you decide to use one of these treadling patterns, you have to be aware of *floats*! You haven't had to be concerned about this issue before, but now that has changed. This can be remedied with the addition of one or more tabby threads. The addition of the tabby keeps the floats a manageable length. If you are working with a larger thread, you may need to add a tabby more often. And of course it also depends on how you will be using your project. If you are making a blanket, it will be even more necessary to keep the floats short. If you are making a table runner, you can allow the floats to be a bit longer.

Thread choice is important when treadling as lace. The color can change, but the size of the weft thread usually looks better if it is the same size as the warp thread. This emphasizes the lace effect. But feel free to experiment and try a larger thread.

I wove a series of samples for both 4-shaft and 8-shaft crackle/lace. The next series of pictures includes a sample woven in white on white and also using a color. This will give you a visual idea of how treadling crackle as lace will look. However, I do suggest that, as with any changes in a project, you should give yourself an extra bit of warp so you can sample to make sure you are getting the look you want. In this book, you will find projects that are woven as lace. These include the Blocks of Thyme Shawl (4 shaft, page 47) and Diamonds and Lace Table Runner (8 shaft, page 103).

First we will look at 4-shaft examples.

In Lace sample 1 (Figures 4.6 and 4.7), you will notice that there are three tabby threads in each block that are the same. The fourth tabby thread is the one that stops the float from being too long. You will want to complete each block, including the odd tabby thread, before repeating that block.

Figure 4.6.
Lace sample 1, 4 shaft.

Figure 4.7.
Treadling for Lace sample 1, 4 shaft.

In Lace sample 2 (Figures 4.8 and 4.9), you will notice that the tabby is not used in this lace treadling. The float is automatically stopped when you change blocks. Feel free to add a tabby thread if you want. It will not impact your design. If you want to repeat a block, you will need to add a tabby thread, as indicated in Figure 4.10. It doesn't make any difference which tabby is used. The important idea is that the float length will be limited by this tabby! In the samples, the blocks were repeated only one time and no tabby threads were used.

Figure 4.8.
Lace sample 2, 4 shaft.

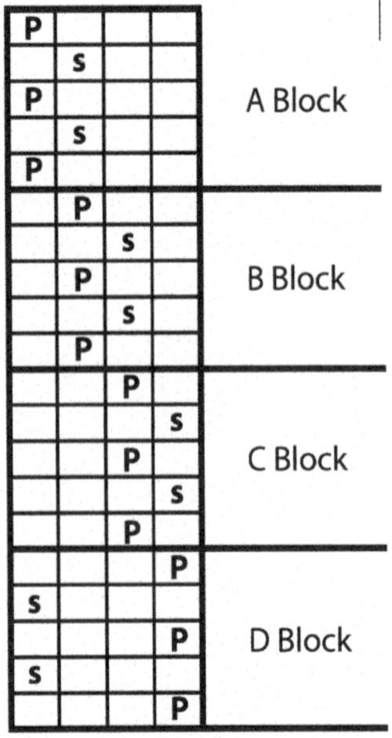

Now let's look at 8-shaft examples.

The first sample (Figures 4.11 and 4.12) is very similar to a 4-shaft treadling except that the additional treadles have been added. Since there are tabby threads, the floats are controlled and do not get too long. Note that you will have three tabby threads between each block. In this sample the weft thread for the pattern and the tabby are the same thread, same size.

Figure 4.9.
Treadling for Lace sample 2, 4 shaft.

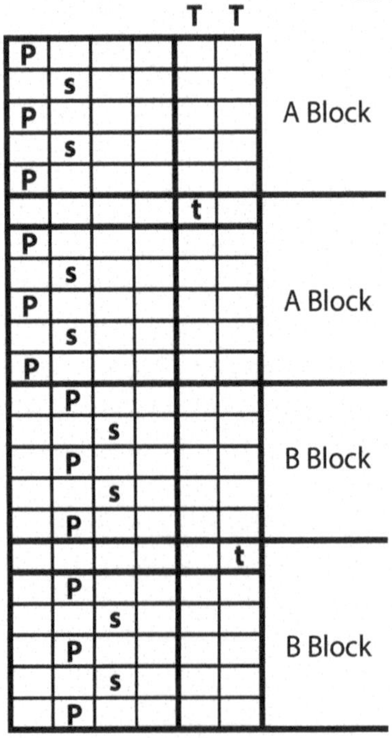

(Figure 4.9 shows treadling draft with A Block, B Block, C Block, D Block marked with P and s symbols.)

Figure 4.10.
Tabby added between repeating blocks.

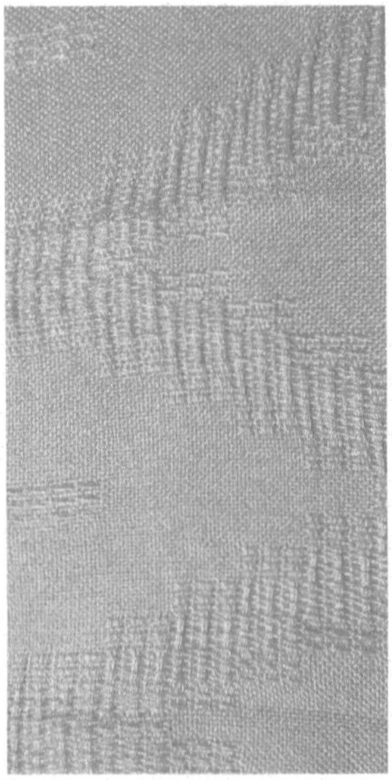

(Figure 4.10 shows treadling draft with A Block, A Block, B Block, B Block marked with P, s, t symbols and T T at top.)

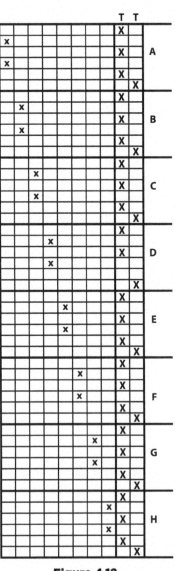

(Figure 4.12 shows 8-shaft treadling draft with blocks labeled A through H, marked with x and X symbols, T T at top.)

Figure 4.11.
Lace sample 1, 8 shaft.

Figure 4.12.
Treadling for Lace sample 1, 8 shaft.

Look closely at the next sample (Figures 4.13 and 4.14), and you can easily spot the vertical floats. In this sample one thread is 5/2 and the second thread is 10/2. Keep in mind that these are samples. Think about how this would look if the threads were the same size. The piece could have a more delicate look. The use of two colors creates a sharper pattern, whereas a monochromatic color scheme is richer and more subtle.

You can repeat any block multiple times, but be sure to add the tabby after each block is completed. It doesn't matter which tabby is used. I have indicated the tabby based on the block repeated only one time. Ideally you will alternate the tabby threads. I always tie up my tabby treadles on the outside. This way I know that if my shuttle is on the right side of my piece, I need to treadle the tabby on the right. And if my shuttle is on the left side of the piece, I need to treadle the tabby on the left. This ensures that I am alternating the tabby throws. Have fun and experiment with weaving crackle as lace.

Figure 4.13.
Lace sample 2, 8 shaft.

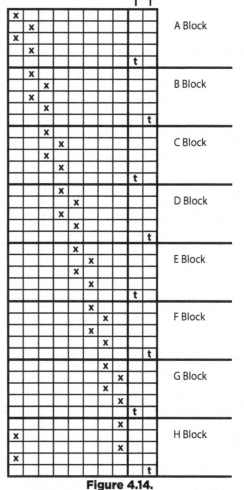

Figure 4.14.
Treadling for Lace sample 2, 8 shaft.

Treadling on Opposites

This is probably the easiest of all of the alternative ways to treadle crackle weave; however, it will only work with 4-shaft patterns. If you remember, you will have a 2/2 twill tie-up, as shown in Figure 4.15. The principle is that you will raise first one set of shafts and then the shafts that make up the opposite set.

Figure 4.15.
2/2 twill tie-up.

The chart in Figure 4.16 shows both the tie-up and the four different blocks you will have when treadling on opposites. In the A Block, you will depress treadle 1, which raises the 1 and 2 shafts. Next you will depress treadle 3, which raises shafts 3 and 4. On opposites!

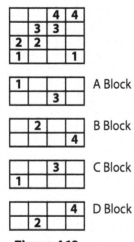

Figure 4.16.
Treadling on opposites.

This is really a very simple idea. The Merry Christmas Runner (page 79) and the Baby Blocks Blanket (page 45) were woven using this technique. You will have two primary threads with this technique. In the projects, the primary threads were twice the size of the warp threads. However, you could use thread the same size as the warp. You do not have to use a tabby for this technique. In the Merry Christmas Runner, the patterned blocks were separated by areas of plain weave as a design element. This is very easy to do since the threading for crackle weave can also be woven as a plain weave.

You could easily combine a textured thread and a smooth thread. Use a textured thread for one pattern

weave and perle cotton for the second pattern thread. Play with color and texture to get the final look you are wanting.

It is easy to see why this method will not work with 8-shaft patterns. Figure 4.17 shows the tie-up for the 8-shaft patterns in this book.

Figure 4.17.
Tie-up for 8-shaft patterns.

There is no combination of treadles that give you an opposite treadling pattern. Don't be discouraged, though. You can still have a lot of fun working only with 4-shaft patterns.

Treadling Crackle as Overshot

This is probably my favorite alternative treadling for crackle. The blocks are crisp and have great definition. It is also an easy method to treadle. Overshot motifs are created by repeating a treadle more than one time. After each pattern thread, a tabby thread is used. These tabby threads anchor any long warp threads and give stability to the woven piece. If you remember, overshot gets its name because the pattern thread "shoots over" the underlying weave structure. It is these floats that create the motif. Crackle floats are no longer than three threads, so treadling as overshot is perfect.

In my samples I was very consistent in the number of repeats of each block. These were just samples. When you weave your piece, you can be more creative. In the Finale Cape (page 107), overshot was combined with twill. But the overshot portion combined two different treadles. The first set of repeats were "2, 2, 1–2, 2, 1–2, 2, 1–2, 2." I could have treadled all "2"s or all "1"s. This was just my choice.

The Cross Vestment (page 57) is another example of treadling crackle as overshot. In this case, the repeats created the image of a cross, which was perfect for its use. The Wavelengths Scarves (page 91) use different numbers of repeats, giving the appearance of movement through the scarves.

Overshot is the perfect way to treadle 8-shaft crackle. The overshot treadling eliminates the undulation that happens if you use traditional crackle treadling. The use of the tabby thread keeps the threads aligned better. Keep this in mind when working with 8-shaft patterns.

Figure 4.18 shows the sample I wove in the overshot style. Figure 4.19 is the treadling graph. In this graph, the numbers indicate how many times a treadle is to be repeated. Remember, each pattern thread is followed by a tabby thread, alternating the tabbies. The tabbies are not shown in overshot treadling graphs. As you can see, here each treadle was repeated eight times and then followed by a tabby thread. Remember, you can repeat as many or as few times as you want.

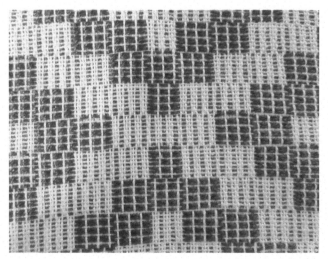

Figure 4.18. Treadling as overshot sample, 4 shaft.

				T	T
4	4				4
3			3	3	
		2	2		2
	1	1		1	
8					
	8				
		8			
			8		
8					
	8				
		8			
			8		
8					
			8		
		8			
	8				
8					
			8		
		8			
	8				
8					

Figure 4.19. Treadling graph for sample.

Figure 4.20 shows the 8-shaft sample woven in the overshot style, followed by the treadling graph in Figure 4.21. In this sample, each treadle was repeated 5 times. Again, that was an arbitrary number. Always remember to follow each pattern thread with a tabby thread, alternating the tabbies. You will notice that there are large areas of plain weave visible in the 8-shaft sample. Keep this is mind when you are designing your project.

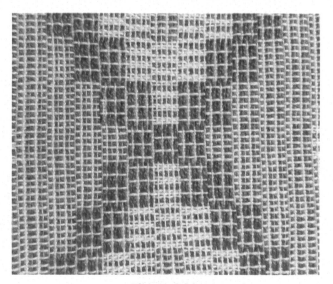

Figure 4.20.
Treadling as overshot sample, 8 shaft.

								T	T
8		8		8			8		8
	7		7			7	7	7	
6		6			6	6			6
	5			5	5		5	5	
4			4	4		4			4
		3	3		3		3	3	
	2	2		2		2			2
1	1		1		1			1	
								X	
									X
5									
	5								
		5							
			5						
				5					
					5				
						5			
							5		
						5			
					5				
				5					
			5						
		5							
	5								
5									

Figure 4.21.
Draft for 8-shaft sample.

The Highlands Table Runner (page 111) is one of the 8-shaft projects that was woven as overshot. I am particularly fond of this pattern and will be re-creating it in another color palette. Another example is the Shadows Table Runner (page 117). When treadled as traditional crackle, the undulation was out of control. Weaving it as overshot solved that problem. Think outside the box, be creative, and have fun using this technique!

Summer/Winter

Summer/winter offers two different ways to treadle your project. The first option is as pairs and the second is as singles.

We will begin with 4 shafts. In summer/winter, a pattern thread alternates with a smaller thread, which is always a tabby. In the following graphs, the "P" is the pattern thread and the "t" is the tabby (or smaller) thread.

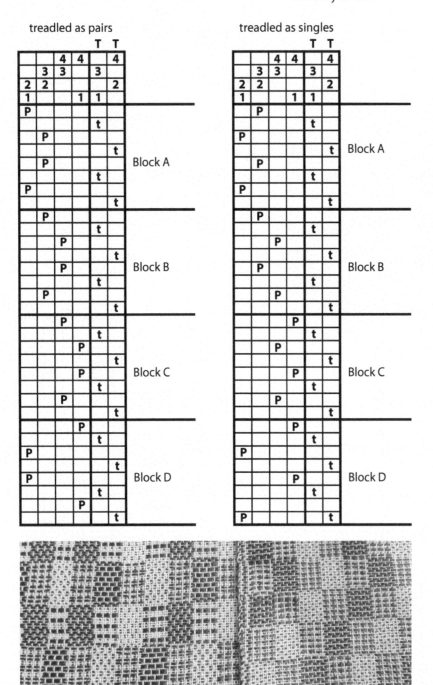

Figure 4.22. These graphs are traditional summer/winter treadling, and each creates a distinct look.

Figure 4.23. The sample on the left is treadled as pairs. The sample on the right is treadled as singles.

Next we will look at 8-shaft summer/winter. The principle is the same.

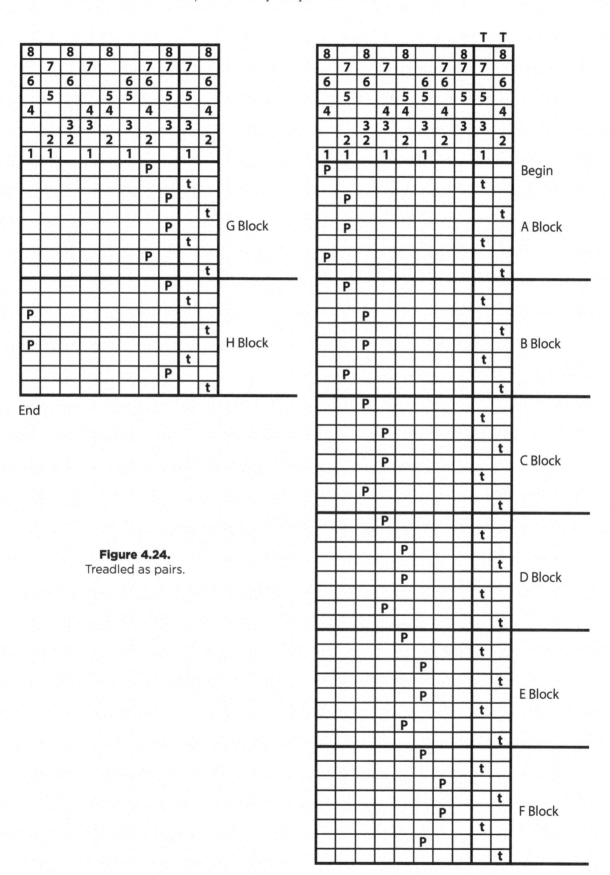

Figure 4.24.
Treadled as pairs.

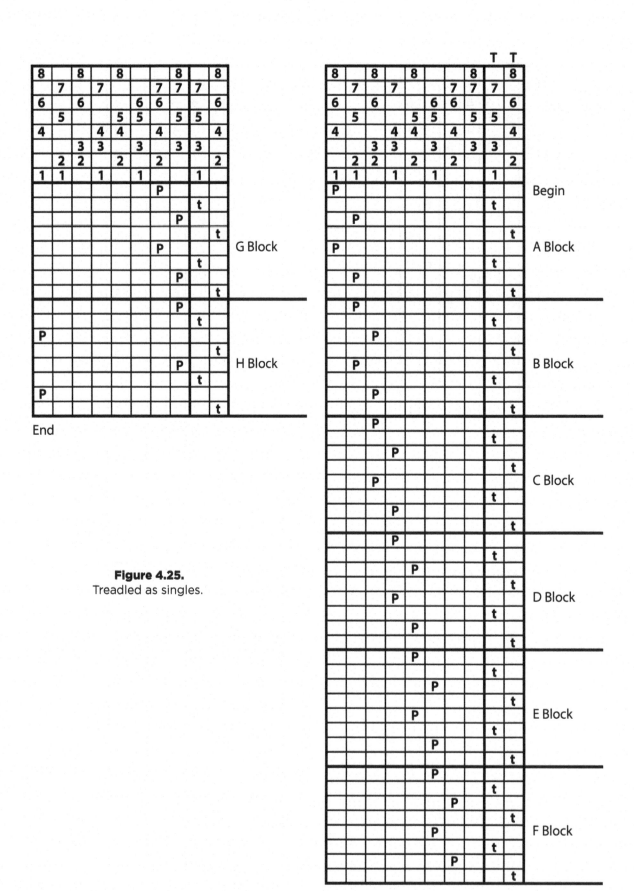

Figure 4.25.
Treadled as singles.

Now let's look at the woven samples (Figure 4.26).

Figure 4.26. The sample on the left is treadled as pairs and the one on the right is treadled as singles.

In each of these examples you will see distinct differences. But every one of them results in a beautiful piece. Remember that weaving true 8-shaft crackle can result in undulation! Weaving your 8-shaft piece as summer/winter is a wonderful option. The use of the true tabby gives the piece structure and prevents the undulations from forming. You can substitute any of these treadling patterns into a crackle weave project.

Treadling as Twill

Crackle weave is a 4-thread point twill following an odd/even threading. This makes treadling a crackle threading as twill very simple. And there are so many options! You can follow a straight twill, M and W, rose path, or a point twill. Or you can combine these different treadling patterns. If you have a computer program, you can put in various treadling patterns and create a new pattern.

Another decision is whether to add a tabby between each pattern thread. Adding a tabby thread opens up the pattern, making it less dense. I wove a number of samples in 4-shaft and 8-shaft using both options and different treadling patterns. Looking at these will help you decide what you like best. It is easy to see which has the tabby thread added.

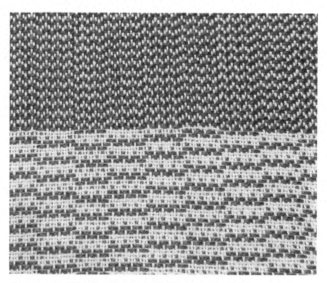

Figure 4.27. 4-shaft straight twill.

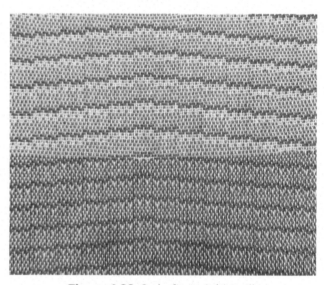

Figure 4.28. 8-shaft straight twill.

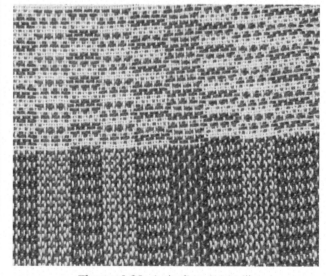

Figure 4.29. 4-shaft point twill.

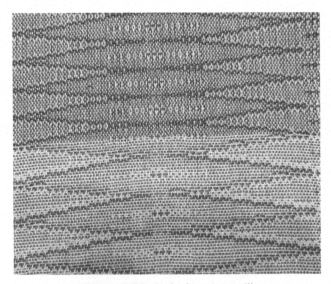

Figure 4.30. 8-shaft point twill.

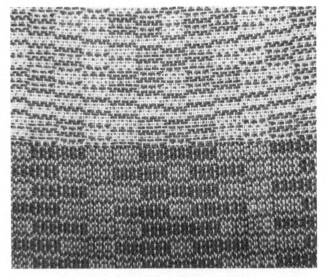

Figure 4.33. 4-shaft M and W.

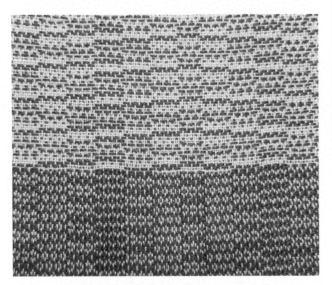

Figure 4.31. 4-shaft rose path.

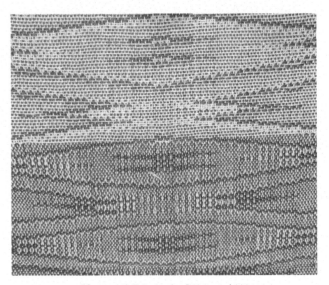

Figure 4.34. 8-shaft M and W.

I have incorporated twills in many of the projects included in this book. The Plum Jellies Dish Towels (page 81) are solely based on treadling as twill. The Blocks of Thyme Shawl (page 47) and Finale Cape (page 107) both include twill treadling as a part of the design. This is your time to try something new!

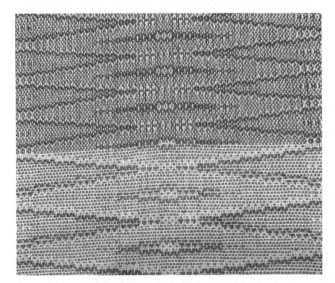

Figure 4.32. 8-shaft rose path.

CHAPTER

5

Color and Texture

Color is such an important part of our weaving process. The finished project can be bold and bright or soft and subdued. Colors evoke emotions in us. When we see blue and pink, we think of babies. A combination of rose and poplin blue reminds us of the 1980s. Yikes, how about avocado green and yellow? That sure dates me! I am sure you can think of many more combinations, ones that are very personal to you. So, let's think about how color and crackle weave combine to create something beautiful.

I want to begin by saying that color choice is not always a place where many weavers are comfortable. A bit of advice here! Building up a good stash of fiber can get costly, which often keeps us from trying new colors and ideas. Lunatic Fringe offers a very affordable twenty-color gamp that provides a wonderful selection of colors plus enough yardages to weave many projects. It is a good place to start and gives you a wonderful palette to work with. All of the projects in this book that use their 10/2 bright colors in the warp have come from the 1.5-oz mini cone size gamp. While it may not appear to have a lot of yarn, it does. I still have fiber left for future projects. You might find that once you have these colors at hand, you will be more willing to take chances. You can always just make samples to see how the colors interact. If you are like me and don't like to sample, just add a bit to the warp length and sample before you begin the final project.

Warp

Color can be added to crackle weave in so many different ways. The most obvious is adding color in the warp. Warps can be composed of one or more colors. I often use two colors of similar value to soften the look of the warp. If I have two partial cones that I want to use up, this is the perfect way to do that. I could combine California Gold and Old Gold for a warp. Since I use a lot of greens, I often combine Scarab and Mint in the warp. I will wind these two threads together and then, when threading the heddles, pick them up randomly. You *can* alternate picking up the colors also. But a word of warning here: If you alternate the colors and make a mistake, it may be very obvious. The random pickup doesn't really have errors. How do I know this? The hard way!

The warp can consist of stripes. Colors chosen can be sleyed and threaded in a definite linear pattern. You might want to have a themed project. For example, a set of dish towels for the holidays might be composed of red, white, and green stripes.

The Shadows Table Runner (Figure 5.1 and page 117) uses individual stripes, in varying widths.

Figure 5.1. The Shadows Table Runner has stripes in the warp.

The Abstract Scarf (Figure 5.2 and page 39) is created with definite stripes. However, in this piece, the colors are so close on the color wheel that the stripe effect is almost nonexistent.

Figure 5.2. The Abstract Scarf is warped in stripes, but the colors used are so similar that the stripe effect is barely visible.

The stripes can also blend into one another. In the Gradation Scarves (Figure 5.3 and page 65), both scarves blend the colors in the warp threads. When moving from one color to the next, there is a section in which the two colors are blended, which eliminates the rigid appearance of stripes. The movement of color is more gradual and is especially effective when mixing two distinctly different colors.

Figure 5.3. In the Gradation Scarves, the two warp colors are blended together at the transitions from one color to the next, avoiding a hard line between colors.

Weft

Crackle weave allows so many different ways to add color through the weft threads. The most obvious is your choice of the pattern thread. Since the pattern thread is twice the size of the warp, it will be the most obvious color in your piece. But the secondary/tabby thread opens up a whole new area to bring in additional colors. Your warp could be white, the pattern thread green, and then you could bring in a purple tone for your secondary thread. Figure 5.4 is a sample of just that. A bonus is that it is another good way to use up some of those partial cones.

Figure 5.4. This piece has a white warp, green pattern thread, and purple secondary thread.

Of course you can always change the color of the pattern thread. In the Jelly Beans Kitchen Towels (Figure 5.5 and page 73), each towel has a different pattern thread color. It's the same warp, but the towels certainly look different.

Figure 5.5. The Jelly Bean Dish Towels share the same warp, but each towel has a different pattern thread color.

You can also change the color of the secondary thread throughout the piece. If you look at the Color Wheel Shawl (Figure 5.6 and page 53), you will see that each 4-block repeat has a different secondary color thread. The sequencing corresponds to the sequence of the warp threads. This changes the colors throughout the entire piece.

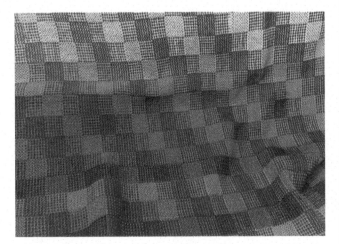

Figure 5.6. Each 4-block repeat of the Color Wheel Shawl has a different secondary color thread, corresponding to the sequence of warp threads.

In the Autumn Table Runner (Figure 5.7 and page 41), you will see this technique again. The secondary threads are the same threads as those in the warp and in the same basic order. When changing the colors of the secondary threads in this manner, you are creating a whole new color. Because the threads are so small, the eye blends the two colors together, creating a third color.

Figure 5.7. The Autumn Table Runner changes the color of the secondary threads in the same basic order as the warp, to cause a visual blending of two colors into a third new color.

Polychrome: More Than One Color!

This is an easy and fun way to use color in weaving, and the crackle weave structure is perfect for this since we are working with blocks. The warp is only one color. The color is introduced through the weft threads. Since there are four blocks for 4-shaft crackle, you will choose four distinct colors. Normally in crackle the pattern thread and the secondary thread are two different sizes. But when working in polychrome, all the threads will be the same size. You have colors A, B, C, and D. In crackle weave Block 1, you will combine Color A and Color B. For this block we will say that A is the pattern color and B is the secondary color. After you have woven that block, you will move on to Block 2 of crackle weave. Now you will put Color A away. Color B becomes the pattern color and Color C becomes the secondary color. In Block 3, put Color B away. Color C becomes the pattern color, and Color D becomes the secondary color. And for the final Block 4, put Color C away. Color D becomes the pattern color, and Color A becomes the secondary color. Now you have worked through all four colors and at the same time you have worked through all four blocks of 4-shaft crackle weave. At this point you can repeat this sequence until your project is finished or, if you want to be really creative, keep adding colors. Look at the Hydrangeas Table Runner (Figure 5.8 and page 69) to see an example of this type of color work.

Figure 5.8. The Hydrangeas Table Runner is made with the Polychrome weaving technique.

Figure 5.9. My husband made these wonderful bobbin holders that I put on my castle when I work Polychrome. It helps to keep the colors in the correct order. It was made from a simple block of wood and quarter-inch dowels. If you make your own, you can add as many bobbin holders as you want. Maybe you have a handy person to help you.

Texture

One final thought: In all but one project the pattern thread was a standard weaving thread, usually 5/2 perle cotton. But let's think outside the box. We can use a knitting yarn and add texture to our piece. The Gold Leaf Scarf (Figure 5.10 and page 63) is an example of this. I used a complementary color for the warp that blended with the chosen yarn. This yarn was made up of three different threads: a variegated nubby thread, a fuzzy yarn, and the gold accent. The gold thread really pops in this piece. Because the yarn is heavier than a 5/2 perle cotton, you will not need very much. I suspect that if you look through your stash, you will find a yarn that you will want to experiment with.

Look closely at this piece! You will also notice that in using the larger pattern thread/yarn, there is a beautiful diamond design created in one of the blocks. Could that be an idea for a future project?

The main point is to play and have fun with your weaving. Don't be afraid to try something new. Put some colors together that you have never done before. Throw in an odd thread that you have on the shelf just to see what happens. It has been my experience that these experiments have turned into something wonderful.

Figure 5.10. Texture is added to the Gold Leaf Scarf by weaving with different types of yarns.

Don't forget thrums (loom waste)! If you look at the Thrum Throw (page 87), you can see that the use of thrums adds both color and texture. Tie the ends of your thrums together to make balls of randomly colored yarn. You can trim the ends or leave them long. Either way, you will have a unique finished piece.

Figure 5.11. Give those textured yarns a try!

Figure 5.12. My thrum basket. Put those loose ends to good use; you'll be amazed at the beautiful results.

Fiber

The bulk of the projects in this book use perle cotton. Why? The main reason is that it is the most common thread that weavers use. Weavers have perle cotton on our shelves. It is easy to obtain, as there are many sources from which to purchase it. And a huge factor is: It is affordable! While I would love to create projects for you with fancy silks, that is something that most of us do not use. And I do want you to try weaving crackle. More experienced weavers can always make the appropriate substitutions.

Be sure to choose quality perle cotton! Purchase fiber that has a high-quality twist and sheen. Not only will you be happier with the final result, but you will also find that a high-quality thread will slide through your reed and heddles easier with fewer tangles.

But also look into other fiber choices. Tencel is a wonderful option for scarves. It has a silky feel and drape that is very pleasing, especially for wearables. I always use a floating selvedge with my projects, but when using Tencel I always double the floating selvedges, two threads instead of one. Weavers have often found that a Tencel floating selvedge shreds or breaks. By doubling the thread, that problem is eliminated. And the use of two threads does not have any effect on the design.

Rug yarn is another wonderful choice for blankets, towels, or rugs. The more it is washed, the softer it becomes. And since it is 100% cotton, it is very absorbent. You could substitute rug yarn as the pattern thread for a scarf. Initially, you might think this would be too heavy. But if the scarf is worn on a cool, crisp fall day, the choice of rug yarn is perfect. Don't dismiss rug yarn simply because of its name! The Thrum Throw is an example, as the thrum balls are made up of rug yarn.

CHAPTER

6

Four-Shaft Patterns

Abstract Scarf

Treadled in Italian Manner

You can have a lot of fun with this scarf. When treadling, I began with eight repeats of each block in the sequence. Then I reduced the repeats to seven, six, five, four, three, and two in each sequence of six blocks. After the two-block repeat, I increased in the same manner back up to eight repeats. I wove to the desired length and was not concerned with finishing with the eight-repeat sections. This was intended to be an abstract or more spontaneous pattern.

This scarf is also a great way to use up those small cones of 10/2 for the warp. I have given you the color sequence that was used for this piece, but if you don't have enough of one color, simply increase the next color or add another color to your scarf. The color sequence does not correspond to the blocks. It is very random.

COLOR SEQUENCE

#10 purple blue	#5 purple blue	#5 purple	#10 purple	#5 red purple	#10 red purple
28 ends	31 ends	31 ends	31 ends	31 ends	29 ends

Have fun with this scarf and make it your own. Play with the colors and repeats until you get the arrangement that you want! Begin and end with 0.5 inch (1.3 cm) of plain weave and hem stitching.

Dimensions: 7.5 x 62 in. (19.1 x 157.5 cm) plus 4-in. (10.2-cm) fringe

Warp

Sett: 24 epi, 12 dent reed, 2 threads per dent

Length: 3-yard (2.7-m) warp

Thread: 10/2 perle cotton, Lunatic Fringe

- #10 Purple Blue, 28 ends, 90 yards (82.3 m), includes 1 floating selvedge
- #5 Purple Blue, 31 ends, 95 yards (86.9 m)
- #5 Purple, 31 ends, 95 yards (86.9 m)
- #10 Purple, 31 ends, 95 yards (86.9 m)
- #5 Red Purple, 31 ends, 95 yards (86.9 m)
- #10 Red Purple, 29 ends, 90 yards (82.3 m), includes 1 floating selvedge

Weft

Pattern thread: 5/2 perle cotton, Astra Bali, 250 yards (228.6 m)

Secondary thread: 10/2 perle cotton, Lunatic Fringe #10 purple, 250 yards (228.6 m)

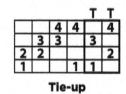

Tie-up

Threading

Border 1: 1 time
Full Motif: 1 time
Border 2: 1 time
Insert appropriate threading for each lettered block.
Incidentals are indicated in green.

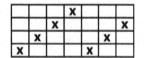

Border 1

Begin

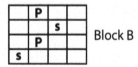

End   **Full Motif**

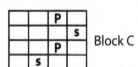

Border 2

Treadling

P = pattern thread
s = secondary thread
Beginning with Block D, substitute the appropriate treadling for each lettered block.

Block A

Block B

Block C

Block D

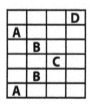

Treadling

Autumn Table Runner

Treadled as Overshot

This is the perfect runner for the fall table! All you need to add is a pumpkin pie, mums, and hot apple cider, and your guests will be most impressed.

This runner is perfect for using up those partial cones of thread, since there is not a lot of yardage required. It would be easy to change the color palette to fit any holiday or just to match your décor. I chose to use three colors, but it would be equally beautiful if you only used one color in the warp. I also alternated the three colors as the tabby thread, changing after I completed the full motif. Think about introducing a fourth color as the tabby thread throughout the whole piece and see what happens!

Feel free to change the number of repeats. You can increase, decrease, or have the repeats increase to the center and then decrease again. There are so many options! Begin and end the runner with 0.5 inches (1.3 cm) of plain weave and hem stitching. If you prefer, weave 1.5 inches (3.8 cm) of plain weave and finish with a rolled hem.

Dimensions: 23 x 44 in. (58.4 x 111.8 cm) with 4-in. (10.2-cm) fringe

Warp

Sett: 24 epi, 12 dent reed, 2 threads per dent
Length: 2.5-yard (2.3-m) warp
Threads: 10/2 perle cotton
- Gold, 176 ends plus 1 floating selvedge = 177 ends, 450 yards (411.5 m)
- Light Rust, 176 ends, 450 yards (411.5 m)
- Light Orange, 196 ends plus 1 floating selvedge = 197 ends, 500 yards (457.2 m)

Weft

Pattern thread: 5/2 perle cotton, Black, 450 yards (411.5 m)
Tabby threads: 10/2 perle cotton
- Gold, 200 yards (182.9 m)
- Light Rust, 200 yards (182.9 m)
- Light Orange, 200 yards (182.9 m)

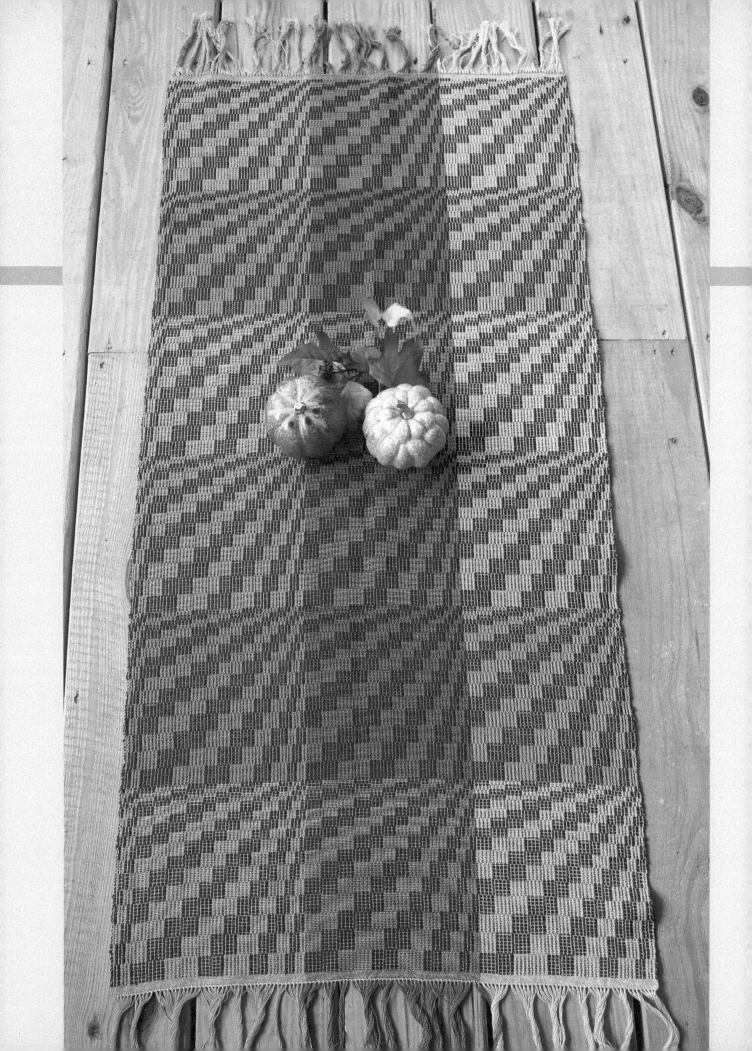

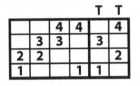

Tie-up

Threading

Repeat Full Motif: 3 times total

End with Partial Motif, if desired:
  1 time

Insert appropriate threading for
  each lettered block.

Incidental threads are indicated
  in green.

Begin

x	D	D	D										x	D	D			x	C	C								x	D			x	C			
				x	C	C	C											x	C	C				x	B	B						x	C			
								x	B	B	B										x	B	B				x	A	A					x	B	
												x	A	A	A																				x	A

x	D	D	D	D												
					x	C	C	C	C							
									x	B	B	B	B			
												x	A	A	A	A

End

Full Motif

x	D				
		x	C		
				x	B
					x A

Partial Motif

Treadling

Repeat full treadling:
  6 times total

Repeat each treadle
  the number of times
  indicated.

Insert a tabby between
  each pattern thread.

T T

2	2			2
		4	4	4
	3	3	3	
2	2		2	
1		1	1	
		t		
			t	
3				
	3			
		3		
			3	
6				
	6			
		6		
			6	
8				
	8			
		9		
			9	
11				
	11			
		12		
			12	

Treadling

Baby Blocks Blanket

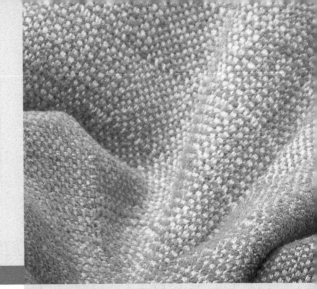

Treadled on Opposites

This baby blanket would be the perfect gift for that special mother-to-be! While this blanket was woven in the traditional pink and blue combination, it would be easy to substitute the colors of your choice. The blanket could match the nursery or just be the favorite colors of the recipient. The size of the blanket is perfect for the newborn but is also large enough to be used for many years. How about making one for that special grandchild?

While this piece was threaded as crackle weave, it was treadled "on opposites." If you look closely at the treadling, you will see that the first color is treadled raising two harnesses. When the second color is treadled, it raises the opposite set of harnesses. It is very easy to get into a rhythm when weaving in this manner.

I had been given numerous cones of a cotton fiber that is similar in feel to terry cloth. I used this for the blanket, which makes it very soft and absorbent. In the requirements I have listed 3/2 perle cotton as a comparable fiber. Cotton bouclé could also work in place of the perle cotton. Any of these fiber choices will result in a beautiful blanket.

Begin and end this piece with 1.5 inches (3.8 cm) of plain weave. Finish this with a rolled hem.

Dimensions: 30 x 45 in. (76.2 x 114.3 cm)

Warp

Sett: 20 epi, 10 dent reed, 2 threads per dent
Length: 2.5-yard (2.3-m) warp
Thread: 5/2 perle cotton, White, 1,600 yards (1,463 m), 599 ends plus 2 floating selvedges = 601 ends

Weft

Comparable fiber: 3/2 perle cotton
- Pink, 475 yards (434.3 m)
- Blue, 475 yards (434.3 m)

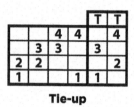

Tie-up

Threading

Insert appropriate threading for each lettered block. Incidental threads are shown in green.

Note that there are twill blocks that need to be repeated 4 times for correct threading.

Begin

Repeat 4X

Border

Repeat 4X

CENTER BLOCK

Repeat 4X

Repeat 4X

Repeat 4X

Repeat 4X

Repeat 4X

End

Border

Repeat 4X

Treadling

P = pink

B = blue

Alternating colors, repeat each block to desired width.

End with Block A for balance.

The baby blanket shown has 8 repeats.

	P		B		**Repeat as desired**
A		P			**Repeat as desired**
B				B	**Repeat as desired**
C	B		P		**Repeat as desired**
D		B		P	**Repeat as desired**
C	B		P		**Repeat as desired**
B		P		B	**Repeat as desired**

Blocks of Thyme Shawl

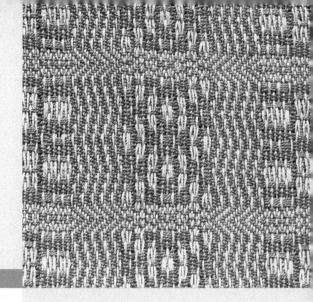

Treadled as Lace

This is a beautiful shawl for any occasion! The use of a light warp with a slightly darker weft in the same color palette gives this piece sheen and elegance. The pattern really shines in the bright sunlight. I can also image this in a combination of white and off-white to be used in a wedding party.

While the threading for this piece is traditional crackle threading, it is treadled in a manner similar to huck lace. Thread choice is very important when designing this piece. There are numerous floats, and as the thread size increases, so does the length of the floats. Ideally, the thread size should not go above 8/2 to prevent fingers or toes from getting caught. Also note that the same size thread is used for both the warp and the weft.

Begin and end this piece with 0.5 inch (1.3 cm) of plain weave and then hem stitching. I chose to do a twisted fringe, but you would not have to if it doesn't suit you.

Dimensions: 23 x 78 in. (58.4 x 198.1 cm)

Warp

Sett: 24 epi, 12 dent reed, 2 threads per dent
Length: 3.5-yard (3.2-m) warp
Thread: 10/2 perle cotton, Jade, 2,000 yards (1828.8 m), 559 ends plus 2 floating selvedge = 561 ends

Weft

10/2 perle cotton, Persian Green, 1,400 yards (1,280.2 m)

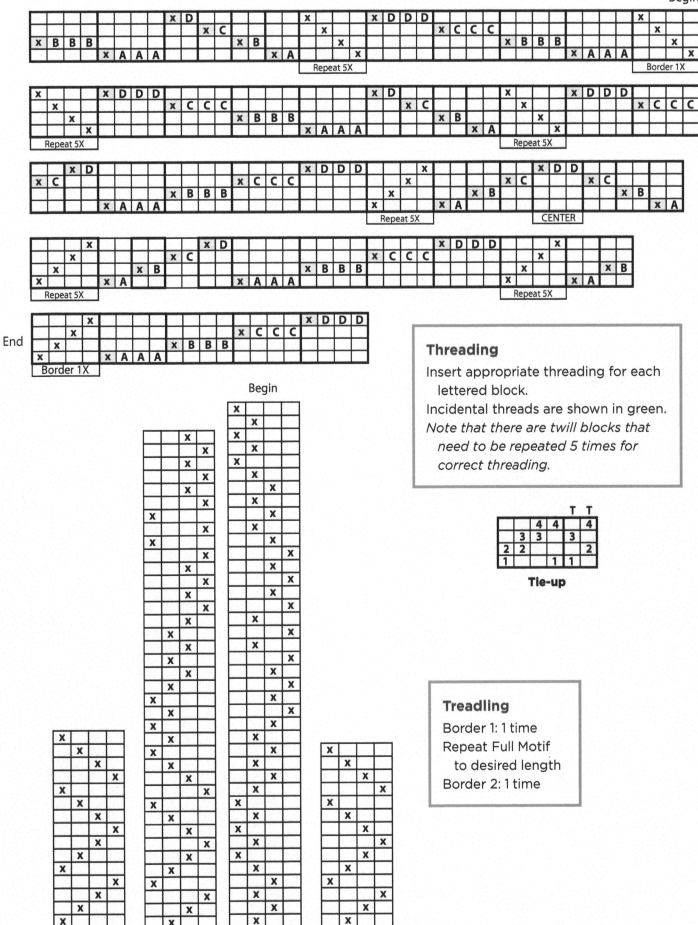

Begin

Repeat 5X

Border 1X

Repeat 5X

Repeat 5X

Repeat 5X

CENTER

Repeat 5X

Repeat 5X

End

Border 1X

Threading

Insert appropriate threading for each lettered block.

Incidental threads are shown in green.

Note that there are twill blocks that need to be repeated 5 times for correct threading.

T T

Tie-up

Treadling

Border 1: 1 time
Repeat Full Motif to desired length
Border 2: 1 time

Begin

Border 2   End   **Full Motif**   **Border 1**

Blue Shadows Scarf

Classic Crackle

A comment I often hear about crackle weave is that it is so busy! But this scarf woven with just one color and one size thread for the pattern and secondary thread really gives a new look to crackle weave. Add to that the richness of the silver gray warp threads, and you have a very rich and sophisticated piece. Can you imagine this done in white on white? That would be a beautiful, elegant scarf.

The use of Tencel also gives the scarf a gorgeous drape. If you have trouble with Tencel floating selvedges breaking, just use two threads on each side instead of one. This step should eliminate any breakage.

Begin and end the scarf with 0.5 inch (1.3 cm) of plain weave and hem stitching. I left the fringe long so I could do a twisted fringe. I find this is the best finish for Tencel, as it has a tendency to fray.

Dimensions: 7.5 x 64 in. (19.1 x 162.6 cm) with 5-in. (12.7-cm) fringe

Warp

Sett: 24 epi, 12 dent reed, 2 threads per dent
Length: 3.5-yard (3.2-m) warp
Thread: 8/2 Tencel, Silver Gray, 675 yards (617.2 cm), 185 ends plus 2 floating selvedges = 187 ends

Weft

Thread: 8/2 Tencel, Blue Gray, 300 yards (274.3 cm)

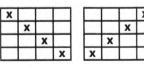

Border 1 **Border 2**

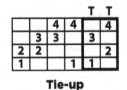

Tie-up

Threading

Border 1: 2 times

Repeat entire threading sequence, substituting the appropriate threading for each lettered block.

Border 2: 2 times

Incidental threads are indicated in green.

Begin

End

Treadling

Begin and end the scarf with the single 4; this will balance the scarf.

Twill pattern: 1 time

Motif: 1 time

Repeat this sequence until desired length.

Finish with Twill Sequence, and then the ending 4.

Incidentals are shown in green.

Substitute the appropriate threading for each lettered block.

Beginning/ending

Twill sequence

Motif

Color Wheel Shawl

Treadled as Summer/Winter Single Bricks

This shawl will really make a statement when you wear it for any occasion. The fiber used was the Tubular Spectrum available through Lunatic Fringe in 10/2 perle cotton. This kit includes twenty different colors and three different ways to position the colors. I chose "Around the Spectrum."

When threading the loom, you will see that the motif is quite simple. It consists of repeating the A, B, C, and D blocks six times with the incidentals included. The main motif is then repeated five times. Each color is assigned to one block: A, B, C, or D. You now have twenty colors and twenty blocks. Feel free to change the placement of the colors if you wish.

Now to the treadling! This shawl is treadled as summer/winter single bricks. Looking at the treadling, you will see that you have an A, B, C, and D block. Within these blocks you will see a "P" and a "t." The "P" stands for the pattern thread. In this shawl, the pattern thread is the 5/2 perle cotton in Black. Each block should be woven to square. In my shawl each block was repeated seven times. You may need to adjust that number.

The "t" is for the tabby thread. This is where you will introduce the color spectrum into the weft. The colors now become the tabby threads. You will follow the sequence that you used in the warp. The complete treadling motif should be finished with one tabby color. Then you start again with the next color in the sequence. This means the tabby color will cover approximately 4 inches (10.2 cm) before you change color. Of course, you can choose to do this differently. Remember the shawl is yours.

Begin and end with 0.5 inches (1.3 cm) of plain weave and hem stitching.

As weavers, we all too often make these wonderful color gamps and then hang them on the wall or cut them up for dish towels. This shawl takes your creation out where it can be seen and admired by everyone.

Dimensions: 24 x 80 in. (61 x 203.2 cm) with 5-in. (12.7-cm) fringe

Warp

Sett: 24 epi, 12 dent reed, 2 threads per dent

Length: 3.5-yard (3.2-m) warp

Threads: 10/2 perle cotton, Lunatic Fringe Color Spectrum

- #10 Blue Green, 30 ends, including 1 for floating selvedge
- #5 Blue Green, 29 ends
- #10 Green, 29 ends
- #5 Green, 29 ends
- #10 Green Yellow, 29 ends
- #5 Green Yellow, 29 ends
- #10 Yellow, 29 ends
- #5 Yellow, 29 ends
- #10 Yellow Red, 29 ends
- #5 Yellow Red, 29 ends
- #10 Red, 29 ends
- #5 Red, 29 ends
- #10 Red Purple, 29 ends
- #5 Red Purple, 29 ends
- #10 Purple, 29 ends
- #5 Purple, 29 ends
- #10 Purple Blue, 29 ends
- #5 Purple Blue, 29 ends
- #10 Blue, 29 ends
- #5 Blue, 30 ends, including 1 for floating selvedge

(continued on page 55)

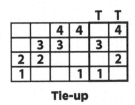

Tie-up

Threading

Refer to the description for color placement.

Insert appropriate threading for each lettered block.

Incidentals are shown in green.

		T		T	
		4	4		4
	3	3		3	
2	2				2
1			1	1	

x	D	D	D	D	D																						
						x	C	C	C	C	C																
												x	B	B	B	B	B	B									
																			x	A	A	A	A	A	A		

Motif
Repeat 5 times

Treadling

Refer to description for complete explanation.

Block A - Repeat to square

Block B - Repeat to square

Block C - Repeat to square

Block D - Repeat to square

(continued from page 53)

The numbers before the color are related to the color and not the size of the thread. Each cone in the kit has approximately 400 yards (365.8 m). For the warp, you will use approximately 110 yards (100.6 m) of each color.

Weft

Pattern thread: 5/2 perle cotton, Black, 800 yards (731.5 m)
Again following the color sequence as in the warp, you will use approximately 10 yards (9.1 m) of each color. (You will be using approximately 120 yards (109.7 m) total of each color, leaving you with enough fiber for another wonderful creation.)

Cross Vestment

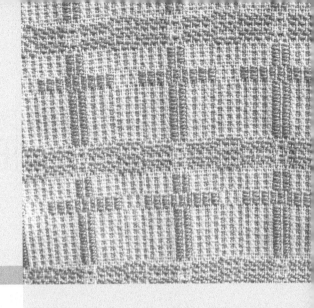

Treadled as Overshot

This vestment would be the perfect gift for your pastor at Christmas or any other special occasion. The crosses are a beautiful Christian symbol that we all understand. The colors could easily be changed to match a season or a particular religious holiday. You could also simplify the design by using the crosses only as a border accent and just repeating the twill for the rest of the piece. Another idea is to do extra repeats of the twill at the midpoint that falls at the neck. This would give emphasis to this area and also a larger break between the cross directions. How about adapting the cross pattern to a table runner or altar cloth?

This vestment is equally beautiful on both sides. The light and dark areas are exactly reversed on each side, which allows the wearer to choose which side they would like to show. Fringe is optional depending on your preference. If you leave fringe, be sure to begin and end with 0.5 inch (1.3 cm) plain weave and then hem stitch. You could also do 1.5 inches (3.8 cm) of hem stitch and finish with a rolled hem.

Dimensions: 7 x 80 in. (17.8 x 203.2 cm) plus 4.5-in. (11.4-cm) fringe

Warp

Sett: 24 epi, 12 dent reed, 2 threads per dent
Length: 3.5-yard (3.2-m) warp
Thread: 10/2 perle cotton, Champagne, 625 yards (571.5 m), 171 ends plus 2 floating selvedges = 173 ends

Weft

5/2 perle cotton, Oak, 375 yards (342.9 cm)
Tabby: 10/2 perle cotton, Champagne, 400 yards (365.8 m)

Threading

Border: 1 time
Full Motif: 3 times
Partial Motif: 1 time
Border: 1 time
Insert appropriate threading for each lettered block.

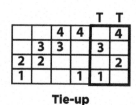

Tie-up

Borders

Full Motif
Repeat this sequence 3 times

Partial Motif to balance

Treadling

Repeat each treadling the number of times indicated.
Begin with the Border; repeat 4 times.
Follow with Sequence A: 21 times (this will be the midpoint)
Follow with Sequence B: 21 times
End with the Border; repeat 4 times.
Add a tabby between each pattern thread.
The charts are read from top to bottom.

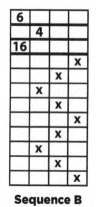

Sequence B

Partial Motif to balance

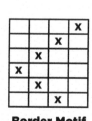

Border Motif
Repeat 4 times

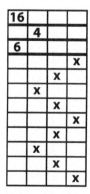

Sequence A

Ebb Tide Table Runner

Treadled as Overshot

I can just picture this table runner at your summer cottage near the lake or ocean! Create a seashell centerpiece to complete the picture. The cool blue color and the movement of the pattern mimic the ins and outs of the tides. Plan an evening buffet with fish tacos and margaritas. It would be sure to please.

This piece is threaded as crackle weave but treadled as overshot. Treadling it in this manner allows the pattern to become more visible. I experimented with treadling it in the classic crackle manner, but the pattern was lost. Begin and end with 1.5 inches (3.8 cm) of plain weave and a rolled hem. Or, if you prefer, just weave 0.5 inches (1.3 cm) of plain weave, and then hem stitch and leave a fringe.

One more note! You will notice that I used two colors in the warp. I have some reasons for that. The first is that using two colors is a wonderful way to add more interest to your piece. They can be similar colors or totally different. Another reason is that this is a good way to use up those partial cones that we all have. And of course, it is always faster to wind two threads at a time!

Dimensions: 18 x 45 in. (45.7 x 114.3 cm)

Warp

Sett: 24 epi, 12 dent reed, 2 threads per dent
Length: 2.5-yard (2.3-m) warp
Threads: 10/2 perle cotton
- Poplin, 219 ends, 575 yards (525.8 m)
- Tyrol, 218 ends, 575 yards (525.8 m)
- 435 ends plus 2 floating selvedges = 437 ends

Weft

5/2 perle cotton, Paradise, 375 yards (342.9 m)
Tabby: 10/2 perle cotton, Poplin, 400 yards (365.8 m)

Threading

Border 1: 1 time
Full Motif: 6 times
Partial Motif: 1 time
Border 1: 1 time
Incidentals are
 indicated in green.
Insert appropriate
 threading for each
 lettered block.

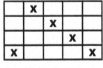

Tie-up

Border 1

Full Motif

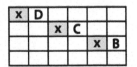

Partial Motif

Border 2

Treadling

Repeat each treadling the
 number of times indicated.
Add a tabby thread between
 each pattern thread.
Repeat Full Motif to desired
 length.
End with Partial Motif.

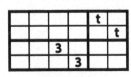

Partial Motif

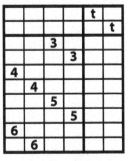

Full Motif

Gold Leaf Scarf

Woven as Summer/Winter Doubles

This is a perfect scarf for that dressy occasion! The sparkle of the gold in the pattern thread gives it a touch of richness. It would be the perfect accent for that little black dress on date night. Change to a different color palette for a totally different and possibly more casual look.

This piece was woven as summer/winter doubles, although you could easily also weave it in the classic crackle manner. The acrylic/mohair blend is used as the pattern thread, and the perle cotton is the tabby thread. Adding a thread like this adds texture to your woven piece. A word of caution: The acrylic/mohair blend is a double-stranded yarn and will take a bit of care getting used to it. Don't overload your bobbin, and you should have no problems.

Since this scarf takes so little fiber, it is a great stash buster. Look through your yarns, and I'm sure you will find the perfect one to make this scarf your own.

Dimensions: 7.5 x 64 in. (19.1 x 162.6 cm) with 5-in. (12.7-cm) fringe

Warp

Sett: 24 epi, 12 dent reed, 2 threads per dent

Length: 3-yard (2.7-m) warp

Thread: 10/2 perle cotton, Oak, 183 ends plus 2 floating selvedges = 185 ends, 600 yards (548.6 m)

Weft

Pattern thread: Lion Brand Moonlight Hair, Safari, acrylic/mohair blend, 2 skeins; 82 yards, 50 grams (75 m, 1.75 oz)

Tabby thread: 10/2 perle cotton, Oak, 150 yards (137.2 m)

Total 10/2 perle cotton, Oak: 750 yards (685.8 m)

Threading

Border 1: 1 time
Motif: 2 times
Border 2: 1 time
Insert appropriate threading for each lettered block.
Incidentals are shown in green.

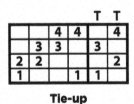

Tie-up

		T	T
	4	4		4
3	3		3	
2	2				2
1			1	1

Border 1

x				x			
	x				x		
		x				x	
			x				x

Motif

x	D	D	D	D	D																	
						x	C	C	C	C												
											x	B	B	B	B	B						
																	x	A	A	A	A	A

Border 2

			x			
		x				x
	x				x	
x				x		

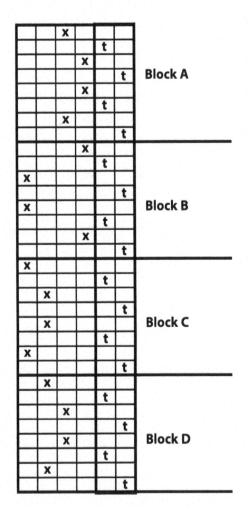

Block A

Block B

Block C

Block D

Treadling

There were 8 repeats of each block in this project. Feel free to adjust as you wish. Weave scarf to desired length.

Gradation Scarves

Overshot or Summer/Winter Singles

Here I've given you a set of scarves emphasizing color gradation. You will notice that in each scarf the warp color is darker on the outside, moving to a light central color. However, they are not set up as stripes. Where the colors join, they are alternated, which make the color change more fluid and gradual. In the scarf with the primary colors, the colors are distinctly different and the mixing of the colors adds new colors. In the second scarf, the orange and yellow palette offers a softer blending of the colors. Remember the Color Wheel Shawl (page 53) made with fiber from Lunatic Fringe? There was thread left on each of the cones. Both scarves were woven from these leftovers, and there is still more left to play with! I did go to my stash for the pattern thread and secondary thread. If you have cones of thread with small amounts, this project could be a great stash buster. Play with the colors you have and see what combinations appeal to you.

I have given you the color sequence using letters instead of the color names so you can substitute your colors accordingly. When you see two letters together, this indicates the blending of the two colors. Simply alternate the colors when threading. In my scarves, when I came to the two colors, I always started with the last color I was working with. So, if I had just threaded the purple/blue section and was beginning on the purple/blue and red blend, I would pick up the purple/blue thread first and then the red thread. Don't get hung up on this step.

Remember that Lunatic Fringe includes a number with their colors. This has nothing to do with the thread size. I also used a floating selvedge with these scarves. This additional thread is included in the thread count.

The treadling for the primary scarf colors is very straightforward. However, the orange/yellow blend has a bit of a twist to it. I treadled the sequence 5 times and then turned the sequence so that both the beginning and the end of the scarf are the same.

I began and ended with 0.5 inches (1.3 cm) of plain weave and hem stitching. I used the 10/2 Champagne thread for the hem stitching as well as the secondary thread.

I used a different treadling technique for each scarf. If you prefer, you could just weave in the classic crackle style or try out any of the other techniques that have been introduced in the book. Have fun!

Gradation: Primary Colors

Dimensions: 7.5 x 62 in. (19.1 x 157.5 cm), 4-in. (10.2-cm) fringe

Warp

Sett: 24 epi, 12 dent reed, 2 threads per dent
Length: 3-yard (2.7-m) warp
Threads: 10/2 perle cotton, Lunatic Fringe
- (W) #10 Purple Blue, 42 ends, 130 yards (118.9 m)
- (X) #5 Red, 54 ends, 175 yards (160 m)
- (Y) #10 Green Yellow, 54 ends, 175 yards (160 m)
- (Z) #5 Yellow, 27 ends, 90 yards (82.3 m)

Weft

Primary thread: 5/2 perle cotton, Soldier Blue, 300 yards (274.3 m)
Secondary thread: 10/2 perle cotton, Champagne, 300 yards (274.3 m)

COLOR SEQUENCE AND NUMBER OF THREADS

X	WX	X	XY	Y	YZ	Z	YZ	Y	XY	X	WX	X
14	14	13	14	13	14	13	14	13	14	13	14	14

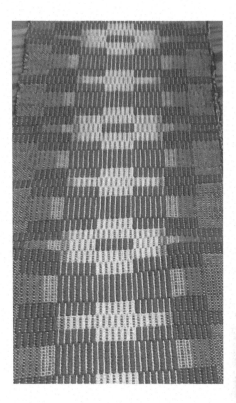

Gradation: Oranges and Yellows

Dimensions: 7.5 x 54 in. (19.1 x 137.2 cm), 5-in. (12.7-cm) fringe

Warp

Sett: 24 epi, 12 dent reed, 2 threads per dent
Length: 3-yard (2.7-m) warp
Threads: 10/2 perle cotton, Lunatic Fringe
- (W) #10 Red, 42 ends, 130 yards (118.9 m)
- (X) #5 Yellow Red, 54 ends, 175 yards (160 m)
- (Y) #10 Yellow Red, 54 ends, 175 yards (160 m)
- (Z) #10 Yellow, 27 ends, 90 yards (82.3 m)

Weft

Primary thread: 5/2 perle cotton, Black, 250 yards (228.6 cm)
Secondary thread: 10/2 perle cotton, Champagne, 250 yards (228.6 cm)

COLOR SEQUENCE AND NUMBER OF THREADS

X	WX	X	XY	Y	YZ	Z	YZ	Y	XY	X	WX	X
14	14	13	14	13	14	13	14	13	14	13	14	14

Begin

Threading (top draft):

																															x	D	D	D	D	D
																								x	C	C	C	C	C								
x	B	B	B	B	B	B											x	B	B	B	B	B	B														
					x	A	A	A	A	A	A																										

End (threading):

x	D	D	D	D	D
					x	C	C	C	C	C	C

End

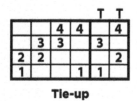

T   T

Tie-up

		4	4		4
	3	3		3	
2	2				2
1			1	1	

Threading

Repeat 1 time.
Insert appropriate threading for each lettered block.
Incidentals are indicated in green.

T   T

Motif A / Motif B

		4	4		4
	3	3		3	
2	2				2
1			1	1	
				t	
					t
	20				
		10			
			10		
10					
			10		
		10			
	20					— Motif A
		10			
			10		
		10				— Motif B

Primary Colors Treadled as Overshot

Alternate Motif A and B to desired length.
End with Motif A.
Add tabby between each thread.

Orange/Yellow Treadled as Summer/Winter Singles

Repeat each block the number of times indicated.
Repeat entire treadling sequence 5 times.
Turning the Design: After the fifth sequence repeat, reverse the sequence beginning with Block D to Block A. Then repeat the entire sequence 4 more times.

Summer/Winter treadling:

		4	4		4	
	3	3		3		
2	2				2	
1			1	1		
	P					
				t			— Block B 8 times
		P				
					t	
			P			
				t			— Block C 12 times
		P				
					t	
			P			
				t			— Block D 16 times
P						
					t	
	P					
				t			— Block A 20 times
P						
					t	

Hydrangeas Table Runner

Classic Crackle

I have a beautiful hydrangea plant in the backyard. It always amazes me that you can get so many different colors of flowers in one plant. My hydrangea delights me with purples, pinks, and blues, just the colors that are in this table runner. This runner would be a stunning addition to any table. Here is another idea: How about changing the color palette completely to make the runner more appropriate for fall or the holidays? There is no limit to the possibilities.

The color sequencing in the runner is referred to as Polychrome. There are two colors in Block A. When moving to Block B, the primary color becomes the secondary color and a new color is introduced. Follow the same sequence when moving to Block C and D. How do you know which is the primary color? The primary color is the color that is repeated two times on the same treadle. So, in Block A the color would be purple, as it is treadled two times on treadle 2. This stacks the purple, making it more prominent. If you look at the other blocks, you can see the same thing happening on treadles three, four, and one. You will also notice that the primary color and secondary color threads are the same size!

I began and ended with 0.5 inches (1.3 cm) of plain weave, which I wove with the Jade color, same as the warp. You can choose any of the other colors if you prefer.

Dimensions: 18 x 50 in. (45.7 x 127 cm)

Warp

Sett: 24 epi, 12 dent reed, 2 threads per dent
Length: 2.5-yard (2.3-m) warp
Thread: 10/2 perle cotton, Jade, 1,100 yards (1,005.8 m), 431 ends plus 2 floating selvedges = 433 ends

Weft

10/2 perle cotton
- Purple Passion, 150 yards (137.2 m)
- Deep Turquoise, 150 yards (137.2 m)
- Fuchsia, 150 yards (137.2 m)
- Sapphire, 150 yards (137.2 m)

10/2 perle cotton (plain weave at beginning and end): 20 yards (18.3 m)

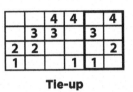

Tie-up

Threading

Repeat Motif 5 times.
Insert appropriate
  threading for
  lettered blocks.
Incidental threads are
  indicated in green.

Motif

pink
purple   Block A
pink
purple
pink - incidental thread

purple
blue   Block B
purple
blue
purple - incidental thread

blue
green   Block C
blue
green
blue - incidental thread

green
pink   Block D
green
pink
green - incidental thread

Treadling

Repeat Blocks A through D
  following the color sequence
  indicated.
Repeat each block to square.
The incidental thread is
  treadled one time after the
  last repeat of the block.
Repeat block sequence to
  desired length.

Jelly Beans Kitchen Towels

Classic Crackle

This is a bright and cheery set of towels for your kitchen. These were created from unmercerized cotton and rug warp, making them a heavier and thirstier towel to soak up all those spills. The multiple colors also hide the stains that will inevitably happen.

The warp uses four colors. I chose green, orange, blue, and yellow. Because you are not using a lot of any one color, this is a great stash buster—an easy way to use up those smaller amounts that we all end up with! I chose the weft in the same manner. I had multiple bits of rug warp, and this was the perfect way to use some of those pieces. That being said, I still have quite a bit left. But the final result is some very nice, heavy towels that will get some great use. These towels would also make a great gift.

You will be treadling these towels in the classic crackle treadling. I used the rug warp as the pattern thread using one color per towel. The secondary thread color changed from block to block, following the color sequence of the warp. If you really want to be colorful, you could use completely different colors.

Begin and end each towel with 1.5 inches (3.8 cm) of plain weave and then a rolled hem.

Dimension: 16.5 x 25 in. (41.9 x 63.5 cm)

Warp

Sett: 20 epi, 10 dent reed, 1 thread per dent
Length: 3-yard (2.7-m) warp
Threads: 8/2 unmercerized cotton
- Green, 84 ends, 275 yards (251.5 m)
- Orange, 84 ends, 275 yards (251.5 m)
- Blue, 84 ends, 275 yards (251.5 m)
- Yellow, 84 ends, 275 yards (251.5 m)

Add floating selvedge at each side matching the colors.

Weft

8/4 cotton rug warp, 150 yards (137.2 m) for each towel
Colors used for projects shown: Red, Navy Blue, and Turquoise, 150 yards (137.2 m) each
Secondary thread: 50 yards (45.7 m) each color
Colors used for projects were same as the warp threads: Green, Orange, Blue, and Yellow

Threading

Repeat pattern 4 times.
Insert appropriate threading
  for each lettered block.
Incidental thread shown in
  green.

T T

		4	4		4
	3	3		3	
2	2				2
1			1	1	

Tie-up

x	D	D	D	D	D														
						x	C	C	C	C	C								
												x	B	B	B	B	B		
																	x	A	A

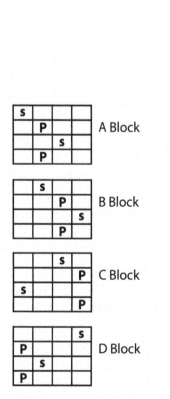

A Block

B Block

C Block

D Block

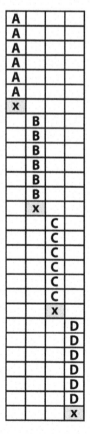

Treadling

Pattern thread is the 8/4
  carpet warp.
Secondary thread: Use
  one warp color per
  block, alternating
  throughout the project.
P = pattern thread
s = secondary thread
Insert appropriate
  threading for each
  lettered block.
Incidental thread shown
  in green.

Just for Fun Mobius Scarves

Summer/Winter and Twill

Have you ever just put on a warp to play with? That is how these two Mobius scarves were created. I put on a generous 3-yard (2.7-m) warp of Jade green cotton. I was intrigued by the fact that treadling the piece as summer/winter would give me a fabric that was definitely two-sided. I used a Noro knitting yarn to give texture to the piece. It was in the process of weaving that I decided that a Mobius scarf would be the perfect way to display both sides. But that would leave a lot of warp, so what to do? The second Mobius was created by treadling a twill pattern and adding a tabby thread in between each pattern thread. This approach opens up the design. If you are using a computer program, you will discover you have lots of options in a treadling pattern, so don't feel that you have to treadle your piece the same way.

I began and ended each piece with 1 inch (2.5 cm) of plain weave. Each end will need to be zigzagged or serged. Twist each piece, placing right side against wrong side. This creates the Mobius twist. Sew the ends together, either by hand or by machine, turning under all raw edges. The picture below shows the two ends joined and ready for sewing together. I prefer to hand sew the ends together, as it makes a softer join. Repeat the process with the second piece.

The seamed edge is worn at the back of your neck with the twist in the front. This is a great way to display both sides of your weaving!

Dimensions: 7.5 x 36 in. (19.1 x 91.4 cm)

Warp

Sett: 24 epi, 12 dent reed, 2 threads per dent
Length: Generous 3-yard (2.7-m) warp
Thread: 10/2 perle cotton, Jade, 179 ends (includes 2 floating selvedges), 575 yards (525.8 m)

Weft

TWILL MOBIUS
Pattern thread: 5/2 perle cotton, Winter Green, 200 yards (182.9 cm)
Secondary thread: 10/2 perle cotton, Jade, 200 yards (182.9 cm)

TEXTURED MOBIUS
Pattern thread: Noro yarn, Menous, wool/cotton/silk blend, Color #3, 131.2 yards (120 m)
Secondary thread: 10/2 perle cotton, Jade, 200 yards (182.9 cm)

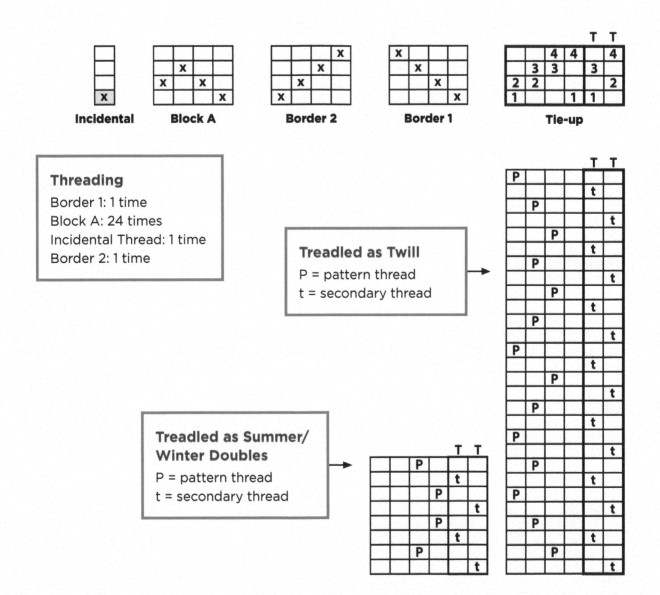

Incidental **Block A** **Border 2** **Border 1** **Tie-up**

Threading

Border 1: 1 time
Block A: 24 times
Incidental Thread: 1 time
Border 2: 1 time

Treadled as Twill

P = pattern thread
t = secondary thread

Treadled as Summer/Winter Doubles

P = pattern thread
t = secondary thread

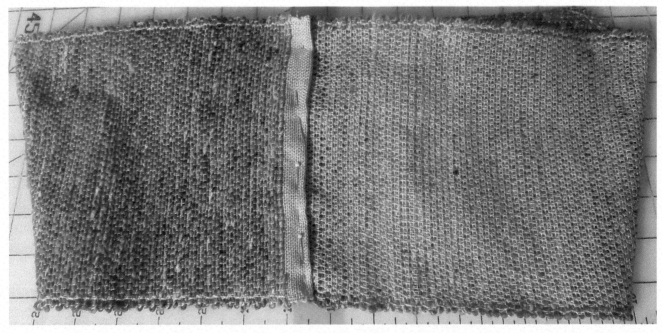

Twist and sew the ends together to form a Mobius scarf.

Merry Christmas Runner

On Opposites

This is a great table runner for the holiday season, and you have so many options when weaving it. I chose to alternate the red and green in the same motif block. For something different, you could alternate white and red or white and green. How about alternating the red and green? Make one stripe in red and one stripe in green. You could easily change the color combination to fit your décor for the holidays. I wrote out the complete threading because of the addition of color, but if you look closely, you can see the crackle weave blocks.

It is a bit tedious when weaving with all the ends to tuck in. But it is worth it in the end.

For the beginning: Weave 2 inches (5.1 cm) of plain weave using white 10/2 cotton.

Now the sequencing begins. Next you will weave the plain weave design using 10/2 cotton in Red, Green, and White:

White: 1 time
Green: 1 time
White: 1 time
Red: 1 time
White: 1 time
Green: 1 time
White: 1 time

Now, using 10/2 cotton, weave 1.25 inches (3.2 cm) of White or to square.

Repeat the plain weave design.

Now weave the Pattern Motif using 5/2 cotton in Red and Green (or as you choose).

This will follow with plain weave design. Notice that the plain weave design frames the pattern motif block.

Repeat this sequence to desired length.

Now to finish: After the last pattern motif block, weave the plain weave design. Then the next 1.25 inches (3.2 cm) of White plain weave, and then the plain weave design one more time. Finish with 2 inches (5.1 cm) of White plain weave, and do a rolled hem at both ends.

Feel free to adjust this pattern to your preferences. Enjoy!

Dimensions: 17.5 x 45 in. (44.5 x 114.3 cm)

Warp

Sett: 24 epi, 12 dent reed, 2 threads per dent
Length: 2.75-yard (2.5-m) warp
Threads: 10/2 perle cotton
- White, 376 ends plus 2 floating selvedges, 378 ends, 1,100 yards (1,005.8 m)
- Red, 15 ends, 50 yards (45.7 m)
- Green, 32 ends, 100 yards (91.4 m)

Weft

10/2 perle cotton
- White, 250 yards (228.6 m)
- Green, 50 yards (45.7 m)
- Red, 25 yards (22.9 m)
5/2 perle cotton
- Red, 100 yards (91.4 m)
- Green, 100 yards (91.4 m)

Threading

Border 1: 1 time
Motif: 11 times
Partial Motif: 1 time
Border 2: 1 time

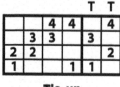

Tie-up

Border 1

Motif

Partial Motif

Border 2

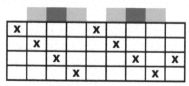

Treadling for Pattern Motif

5/2 cotton

Plum Jellies Dish Towels

Treadled as Twill

Remember when your mother or grandmother used to make plum jelly or jam in the spring? I sure do! The smell in the kitchen was amazing! I always looked forward to that first piece of toast with butter and that fresh jam. There was nothing quite like it!

The jam was a deep purple and had a bit of pink froth on the top that just hadn't quite settled back in. These jars of jam were wonderful to pull out in the cold winter months to remind us that summer would once again return.

This set of dish towels will be perfect in any kitchen. Change the colors to match your décor. You could make a set for the perfect wedding gift. They would really be appreciated!

These towels are threaded as a crackle weave but treadled as a twill. The pattern thread was repeated two times to allow the pattern to be more prominent. This can be easily changed to create the effect you want. Note that a tabby thread is used with this treadling. This opens up the design! Begin and end each towel with 1.5 inches (3.8 cm) of plain weave and a rolled hem.

Dimensions: 16 x 22 in. (40.6 x 55.9 cm)

Warp

Sett: 24 epi, 12 dent reed, 2 threads per dent
Length: 3-yard (2.7-m) warp
Threads: 10/2 perle cotton
- Light Pink, 208 ends plus 2 floating selvedges = 210 ends, 650 yards (594.4 cm)
- Wine, 207 ends, 650 yards (594.4 cm)

Weft

5/2 perle cotton, White, 750 yards (685.8 m)
Tabby: 10/2 perle cotton, Light Pink, 750 yards (685.8 m)

Total light pink: 1,400 yards (1,280.2 m)

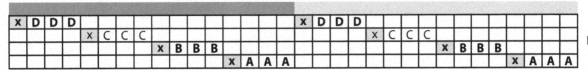

Begin

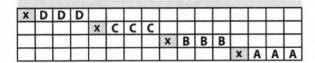

End

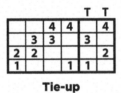

Tie-up

Threading

Begin the threading at the top right at "Begin."

Thread each row, ending with the last row at "End."

Insert appropriate threading for each lettered block.

Incidentals are indicated in green.

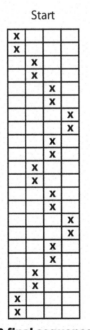

Start

C Treadling
Repeat as desired

B final sequence to balance

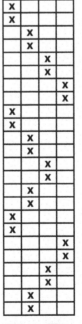

B Treadling
Repeat as desired

Treadling

Pattern thread: 5/2 white cotton

Tabby thread: 10/2 pink

Important: Insert tabby after each pattern thread.

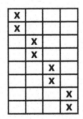

A Treadling
Repeat as desired

Stepping Stones Rug

Classic Crackle

This rug is just the right size for a bathroom or kitchen. As the design progressed through the piece, it reminded me of the stepping stones outside my front door. While I chose blue and green for my accent colors, you could easily substitute colors that would highlight any room in your home.

Black flannel might seem an unusual choice for the fabric, but I was working on this piece while we were all social distancing. Originally, I had thought black cotton, but this material was what was available (or, should I say, on my shelf). When the project was finished, I was very pleased with the feel of this rug. The flannel has made it a very soft rug. This is something to consider when choosing your fabric. Where will you put this rug? Bathroom? Child's room? Flannel would be the perfect choice for these two rooms. You can easily change the colors and fabric to fit your project!

This rug was woven in the classic crackle weave style. Begin and end this rug with 1.5 inches (3.8 cm) of plain weave and a rolled hem.

Dimensions: 22 x 50 in. (55.9 x 127 cm)

Warp

Sett: 12 epi, 12 dent reed, 1 thread per dent
Length: 3-yard (2.7-m) warp
Threads: 8/4 cotton rug warp
- Lime, 136 ends plus 1 floating selvedge = 137 ends, 425 yards (388.6 m)
- Gray Blue, 136 ends plus 1 floating selvedge = 137 ends, 425 yards (388.6 m)

Weft

4 yards (3.7 m) cotton flannel, black; wash and dry, tear into 1-in. (2.5-cm) strips
Tabby: 8/4 cotton rug warp
- Lime, 150 yards (137.2 m)
- Gray Blue, 150 yards (137.2 m)

Total: 575 yards (525.8 m) of each color rug warp

Threading

Substitute the appropriate threading for each lettered block. Incidental threads are indicated in green.

		T	T		
		4	4		4
	3	3		3	
2	2				2
			1	1	

Tie-up

x	D	D	D	D															
					x	C	C	C	C										
										x	B	B	B	B					
															x	A	A	A	A

Threading
Repeat 4 times

Treadling

	s			
A		P		3X
			s	
		P		
	s			
		s		
B			P	3X
				s
			P	
		s		
			s	
C		s		P	3X
				P	
			s		
				s	
D	P				3X
		s			
	P				
				s	

Treadling

P = pattern thread
s = secondary thread
Repeat this whole sequence alternating the tabby colors until you get your desired length.
Begin and end your rug with two inches of plain weave to make a rolled hem.

Thrum Throw

Classic Crackle

This was such a fun piece! As weavers, we all have those thrums (loom waste) when we have completed a project. I truly hate to throw those away! Often, we'll tie them together and just weave dish towels with them. But how about this for a project—a wonderful, soft throw!

I tied numerous rug warp thrums together, mixing up the colors as I went. I did not worry about cutting the tied ends, although you can do that if you choose. Then, for the pattern thread, I used the rug warp thrums. I will admit, it was an experiment when I started, but I love the result. Rug warp often gets a bad reputation, but when it is washed it is the softest fiber. This throw would be ideal to cover your legs on a cool evening. It would also be a perfect baby blanket.

I have given the yardage required as if you were using one color of rug yarn. For this project I tied the thrums together and weighed the balls. I calculated the yardage by taking 75% of the weight as the usable length. In my case, this amount was very generous. The only unfortunate thing is that I didn't use as many of the balls as I had hoped. I guess there will be more throws in my future.

Begin and end the throw with 1.5 inches (3.8 cm) of plain weave and finish with a rolled hem.

Dimensions: 34 x 45 in. (86.4 x 114.3 cm)

Warp

Sett: 20 epi, 10 dent reed, 2 threads per dent
Length: 2.5-yard (2.3-m) warp
Thread: 5/2 perle cotton, Flaxen, 1,800 yards (1,645.9 m), 689 ends plus 2 floating selvedges = 691 ends

Weft

5/2 perle cotton, 500 yards (457.2 m)
Rug warp 4/8, 500 yards (457.2 m)

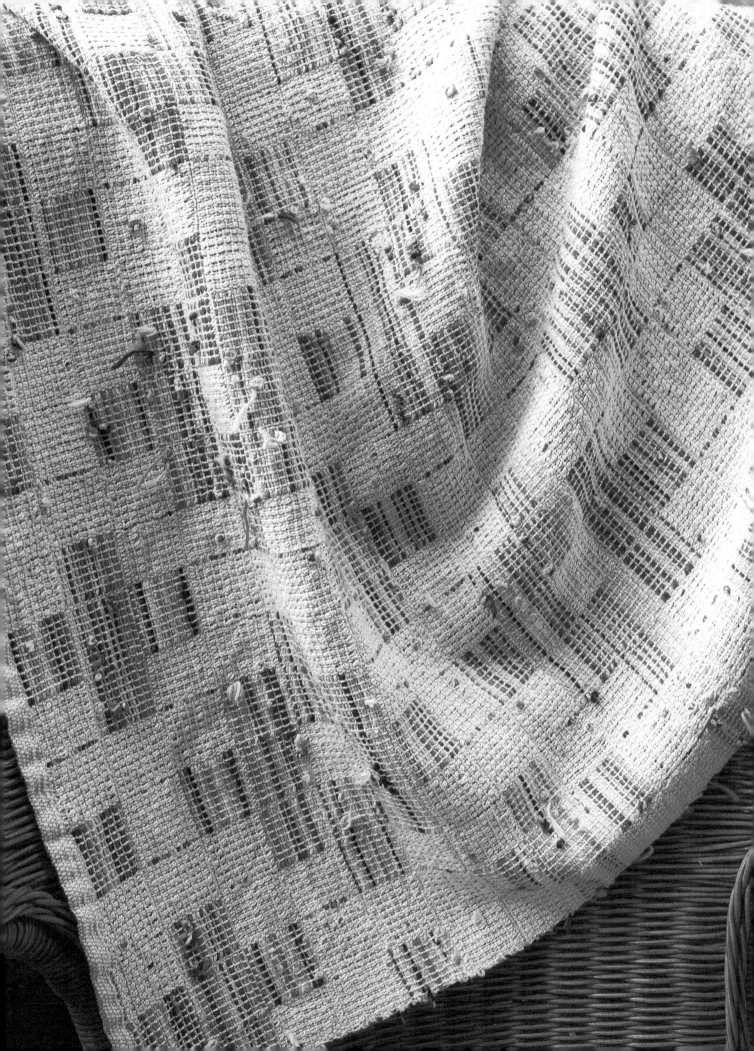

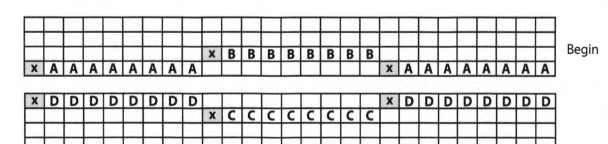

Begin

Motif

End

Partial Motif

Tie-up

			T	T
		4	4	
				4
	3	3		3
2	2			2
1			1	1

Threading

Full Motif: 3 times
End with Partial Motif: 1 time
Insert appropriate threading
  for each lettered block.
Incidental threads are shown
  in green.

Treadling

Repeat Column A and B: 4 times
End with Column A: 1 time
The pattern thread is the thrums.
Insert appropriate treadling for
  each lettered block.
Incidentals are shown in green.

Column B

A		
A		
A		
A		
A		
A		
A		
A		
X		
	B	
	B	
	B	
	B	
	B	
	B	
	B	
	B	
	X	
A		
A		
A		
A		
A		
A		
A		
A		
X		

Column A

		D
		D
		D
		D
		D
		D
		D
		D
		X
	C	
	C	
	C	
	C	
	C	
	C	
	C	
	C	
	X	
		D
		D
		D
		D
		D
		D
		D
		D
		X

Wavelengths Scarves

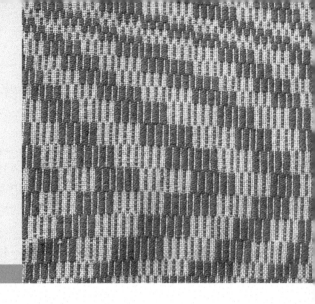

Treadled as Overshot

I love these two scarves! The first time I saw this pattern, I found it hard to believe that it was crackle weave. The way the design moves through the scarves is such a wonderful visual image. One of the designs snakes back and forth; the other design snakes from left to right. Both are definitely attention-getters.

The threading is a crackle weave threading. The treadling is where things change. These scarves are treadled "overshot" style. Notice how the treadling throws are repeated numerous times. Just like in an overshot design! Just make sure that you insert a tabby throw after each pattern throw. Begin and end each scarf with 0.5 inch (1.27 cm) of plain weave and hem stitching. Your fringe can be as long as you like!

The use of Tencel for these scarves gives them a beautiful drape and soft feel. Perfect to wear around your neck in any season!

Wavelengths: Fire

Dimensions: 7 x 62 in. (17.8 x 157.5 cm) with 4-in. (10.2-cm) fringe

Warp

Sett: 24 epi, 12 dent reed, 2 threads per dent
Length: 3-yard (2.7-m) warp
Thread: 8/2 Tencel, Fire, 550 yards (502.9 cm), 173 ends plus 2 floating selvedges = total 175 ends

Weft

5/2 perle cotton, Gold, 275 yards (255.1 m)
Tabby: 8/2 Tencel, Fire, 275 yards (255.1 m)

Total Fire Tencel: 825 yards (754.4 m)

Wavelengths: Pale Lime

Dimensions: 7 x 62 in. (17.8 x 157.5 cm) with 4-in. (10.2-cm) fringe

Warp

Sett: 24 epi, 12 dent reed, 2 threads per dent
Length: 3-yard (2.7-m) warp
Thread: 8/2 Tencel, Pale Lime, 550 yards (502.9 m), 173 ends plus 2 floating selvedges = 175 ends

Weft

5/2 perle cotton, Dark Green, 275 yards (251.5 m)
Tabby: 8/2 Tencel, Pale Lime, 275 yards (251.5 m)

Total Pale Lime Tencel: 825 yards (754.4 m)

Wavelengths tie up and threading

Border 1: 1 time
Threading sequence: 1 time
Border 2: 1 time
Insert appropriate threading for each letter block.
Incidental threads are indicated in green.

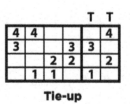

Tie-up

Begin

Threading Sequence

End

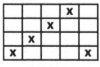

Border 1 **Border 2**

Treadling for Wavelengths in Gold

Repeat A to D treadling sequence to desired length.
End with A for balance.
Use tabby between each pattern row.

Treadling for Wavelengths in Green

Repeat treadling sequence to desired length.
Use tabby between each pattern row.

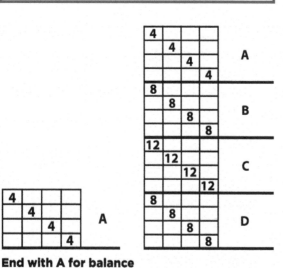

End with A for balance

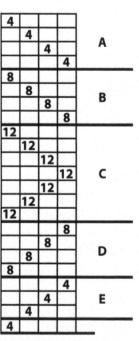

Balance last repeat

Woodland Path Table Runner

Classic Crackle

This table runner really makes a statement! The combination of the greens and brown gave me the feeling of a walk in the woods. This is a perfect runner for the outdoor person. Don't feel like you need to stay with these colors. It would be an equally beautiful runner if it were woven in blues and greens. Think about using pastels in the warp and white for the pattern thread—another unique but beautiful combination!

This is a long runner, but it can easily be shortened by leaving out one repeat. Another way to shorten it would be to reduce the number of repeats in Motif B. Make this runner your own with any changes.

Begin and end the runner with 0.5 inch (1.27 cm) of plain weave and then hem stitch. Or, if you prefer, you can weave 1.5 inches (3.8 cm) of plain weave and finish with a rolled hem.

Dimensions: 17 x 50 in. (43.2 x 127 cm) with 4-in. (10.2-cm) fringe

Warp

Sett: 24 epi, 12 dent reed, 2 threads per dent
Length: 2.5-yard (2.3-m) warp
Threads: 10/2 perle cotton
- Mint, 306 ends plus 2 floating selvedges, 800 yards (731.5 m)
- Oak, 137 ends, 500 yards (457.2 m)

Weft

5/2 perle cotton, Dark Green, 350 yards (320 m)
10/2 perle cotton, Oak, 350 yards (320 m)

Threading

Border 1: 1 time

Alternate Motif A and B: 3 times

Motif A: 1 time

Border 2: 1 time

Insert appropriate threading for each lettered block.

Incidental threads are indicated in green.

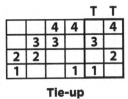

Tie-up

Border 1

Motif A

Motif B

Border 2

Motif B

B		
B		
B		
B		
B		
B		
B		
B		
B		
B		
B		
B		
B		
B		
B		
x		
	C	
	C	
	C	
	C	
	C	
	x	
B		
B		
B		
B		
B		
B		
B		
B		
B		
B		
B		
B		
x		

Motif A

A			
A			
A			
A			
A			
x			
	B		
	B		
	B		
	B		
	B		
	x		
		C	
		C	
		C	
		C	
		C	
		x	
			D
			D
			D
			D
			D
			x
	B		
	B		
	B		
	x		
			D
			D
			D
			D
			x
		C	
		C	
		C	
		C	
		C	
		x	
	B		
	B		
	B		
	B		
	B		
	x		
A			
A			
A			
A			
A			
x			

Border

		B
		B
		B
		B
		B
		x

Treadling

Border: 1 time

Alternate Motif A and B:
   4 times

Motif A: 1 time

Border: 1 time

Insert appropriate
   threading for each
   lettered block.

Incidental threads are
   indicated in green.

Wrapped in Gingham Scarf

Classic Crackle

This scarf is the perfect accent piece for that casual day out. Coordinate this with your favorite pair of blue jeans and a white shirt, and you are ready for any occasion. You could easily substitute your favorite palette of colors such as greens or purples. It would be equally stunning.

The key to this pattern is the color change in both the warp and the weft. The warp has a set color arrangement. When you start to treadle this scarf, alternate the colors as secondary threads, beginning with the darkest blue (Paradise), followed by Poplin, and finish with White. Repeat this sequence until you get the desired length. I ended with the darkest blue for balance.

Begin and end the scarf with 0.5 inch (1.3 cm) of plain weave and hem stitching. Fringe can be any length you desire. I chose 4 inches (10.2 cm) for my scarf!

Dimensions: 7 x 62 in. (17.8 x 157.5 cm) with 4-in. (10.2-cm) fringe

Warp

Sett: 24 epi, 12 dent reed, 2 threads per dent
Length: 3-yard (2.7-m) warp
Threads: 10/2 perle cotton
- White, 52 ends, 175 yards (160 m)
- Poplin (medium color), 52 ends, 175 yards (160 m)
- Paradise (darker color), 65 ends plus 2 floating selvedges = 67 ends, 215 yards (196.6 m)

Weft

Pattern thread: 5/2 perle cotton, Soldier Blue, 200 yards (182.9 m)
Secondary thread: 10/2 perle cotton
- White, 75 yards (68.6 m)
- Poplin, 75 yards (68.6 m)
- Paradise, 75 yards (68.6 m)

Threading

Insert appropriate threading for each lettered block.

Incidental threads are shown in green.

				T	T
		4	4		4
	3	3		3	
2	2				2
1			1	1	

Tie-up

	x				x				x			
		x				x				x		
			x				x				x	
x				x				x				x

Border 1

Begin

x	D	D	D																					x	D	D	D								
				x	C	C	C													x	C	C	C												
								x	B	B	B					x	B	B	B													x	B	B	B
												x	A	A	A													x	A	A	A				

x	B	B	B				
				x	A	A	A

End

			x				x				x	
		x				x				x		
	x				x				x			
x				x				x				x

Border 2

Treadling

Insert appropriate treadling for each lettered block.

Repeat treadling sequence to desired length.

Change the secondary thread color after each complete repeat, following the color sequence of the threading.

A			
A			
A			
x			
	B		
	B		
	B		
	x		
		C	
		C	
		C	
		x	
			D
			D
			D
			x

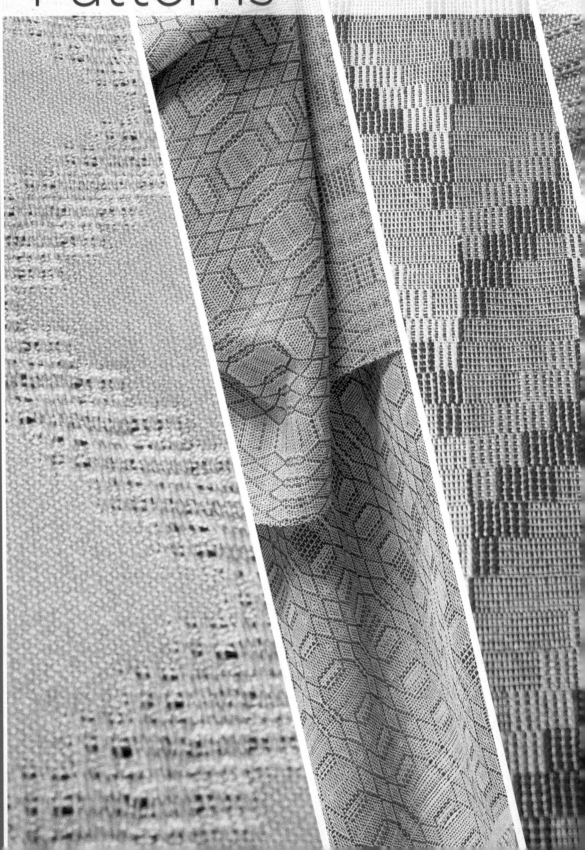

Eight-Shaft
Patterns

Diamonds and Lace Table Runner

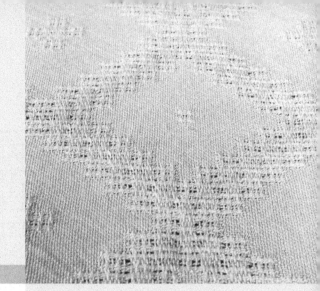

Treadled as Lace

This would be a wonderful runner for a special occasion. Did you have any idea that a crackle weave tie-up could create such a beautiful lace pattern? I chose to do this runner in a neutral color, but it would be equally stunning in blue, green, or gold. There are so many options.

The warp and weft threads are the same size for this project, so there will be only one shuttle to work with. Each block is repeated two times with the doubled tabbies outlining the lace floats. Feel free to change this if you like. Remember, this is your runner!

It is very important to note that where you see two tabbies in a row, the second tabby prevents the lace float from becoming too long. Something else that you must be aware of is that when changing from one block to the next, such as Block A to Block B, the last tabby of that block will be the first tabby of the next block. This will be easy to catch onto because otherwise you would have two identical tabbies in a row. Begin and end the runner with 1.5 inches (3.8 cm) of plain weave and a rolled hem. You could leave fringe if you prefer.

Dimensions: 16.5 x 40 in. (41.9 x 101.6 cm)

Warp

Sett: 24 epi, 12 dent reed, 2 threads per dent
Length: 2.5-yard (2.3-m) warp
Thread: 10/2 perle cotton, Natural, 1,100 yards (1,005.9 m), 402 ends plus 2 floating selvedges = 404 ends

Weft

10/2 perle cotton, Natural, 600 yards (548.6 m)

Threading

Border 1: 1 time
Full Motif: 3 times
Partial Motif: 1 time
Border 2: 1 time
Insert appropriate threading for each lettered block.

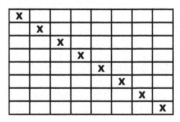

Tie-up

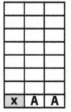

Border 1

Begin

End

Partial Motif

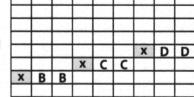

Full Motif

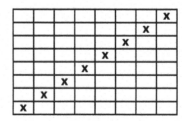

Border 2

Treadling

Repeat each block 2 times in the following sequence—H, G, F, E, D, C, B, A, B, C, D, E, F, G—6 times. End the last repeat with Block H for balance.

When changing from one block to the next, the last tabby of that block will be the first tabby of the next block.

T T

8		8		8	8				8
	7			7	7			7	7	
6		6	6			6			6
	5	5			5		5	5	
4	4			4		4			4
3			3		3		3	3	
	2		2		2	2		2
1		1		1	1		1	

H

G

F

E

D

C

B

A

Treadling

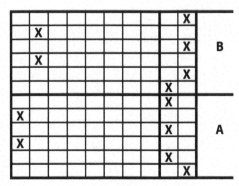

Finale Cape

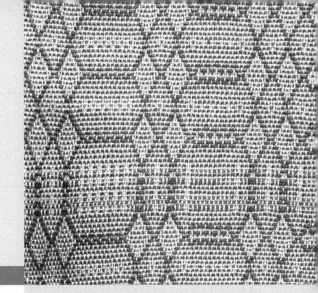

Treadled as Twill and Overshot

This piece is beautiful—a little bit tedious to thread and treadle, but oh, so worth it! This cape is created from two 60-inch (152.4-cm) woven pieces sewn together. Make sure as you treadle that you keep your beat consistent since it will be necessary to match the motif at the seam. I keep a measuring tool handy and write down how long each unit is so when I do that unit the second time I can measure for accuracy. Sometimes it may be necessary to unweave a portion so that the motifs match. When you get your pieces woven, finish with the twisted fringe, and then wash. Then carefully seam them together. You can hand stitch them together or make a tiny seam on the sewing machine using a walking foot. Pin the pieces together and drape over your shoulders so you know where to end the seam. I like to take the joined pieces to the sewing machine and put a row of stitching at the section where the stitching ends. This is a weak point and will pull over time. The row of stitching reinforces this area and helps to prevent the pulling.

Both sides of these pieces are attractive, so you may decide once you get them off the loom that you want to highlight the reverse side. With careful seaming, the cape can be reversed on a whim.

If you don't want to create two pieces, just adjust the length of the warp and make one long shawl. Any way you go, you will have something beautiful to wear.

Dimensions: 2 pieces each 20.5 x 60 in. (52.1 x 152.4 cm), with 4-in. (10.2-cm) fringe

Warp

Sett: 24 epi, 12 dent reed, 2 threads per dent
Length: 5-yard (4.6-m) warp
Thread: 10/2 perle cotton, Stone, 497 ends plus 2 floating selvedges = 499 ends, 2,500 yards (2286 m)

Weft

5/2 perle cotton, Soldier Blue, 1,400 yards (1280.2 m)
Tabby: 10/2 perle cotton, Stone, 1,400 yards (1280.2 m)

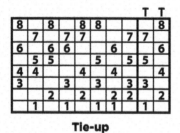

Tie-up

Threading

Repeat entire threading
one time.
Insert appropriate
threading for each
lettered block.

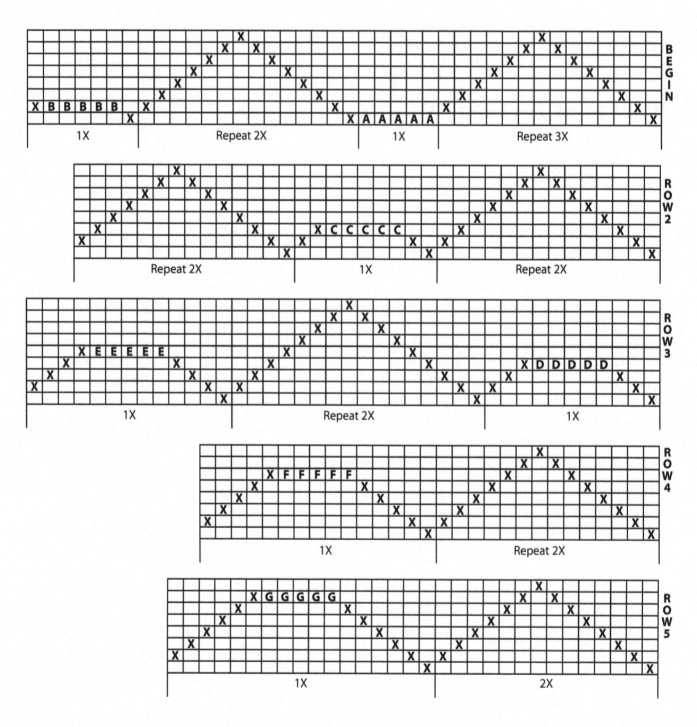

continued

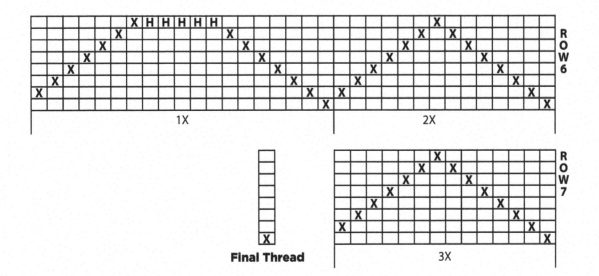

Final Thread

ROW 6

1X   2X

ROW 7

3X

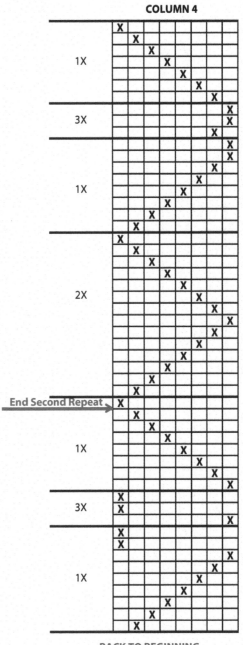

COLUMN 4

1X

3X

1X

2X

End Second Repeat

1X

3X

1X

BACK TO BEGINNING

Treadling

Columns are read top down.
Work Columns 1–4.
Repeat, ending where
  indicated on Column 4.

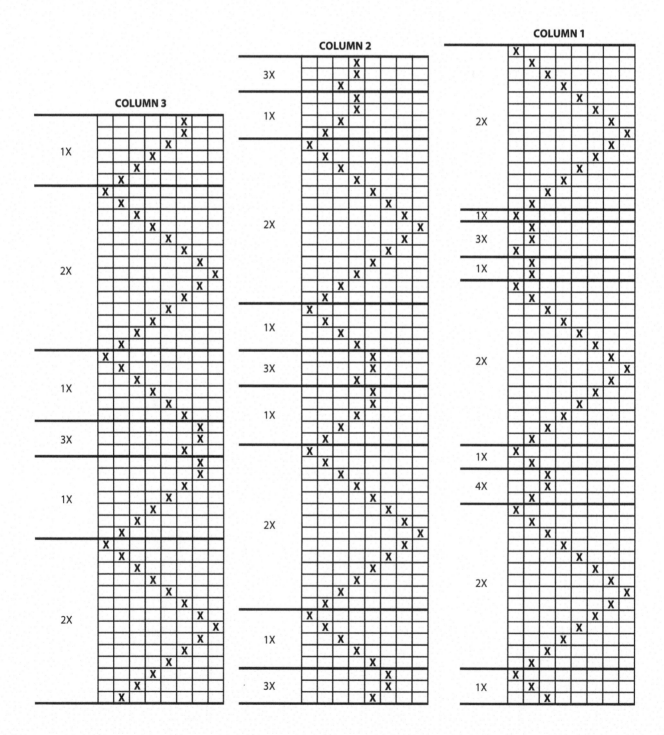

Highlands Table Runner

Treadled as Overshot

So many times when planning a threading pattern, we follow a standard sequence: A followed by B, B followed by C, and so on. This time I mixed things up a bit. This breaks the pattern and makes a very interesting design. However, since I still had to maintain the odd/even rule, you will find that there are some extra incidental threads. I still indicate those in green so that they will be very visible to you. Begin and end the runner with 1.5 inches (3.8 cm) of plain weave and a rolled hem. You can leave fringe if you prefer.

Adding a striped warp also adds more interest to the design. I chose to use two colors, but you could easily add additional colors to the warp. If you wish to have a wider piece, add another repeat of one of the blocks or just increase within each repeat. Reverse this approach to decrease the repeats if you wish to make a scarf. Adapt the pattern to make the project your own.

Dimensions: 16.5 x 45 in. (41.9 x 114.3 cm)

Warp

Sett: 24 epi, 12 dent reed, 2 threads per dent
Length: 2.5-yard (2.3-m) warp
Threads: 10/2 cotton
- Flaxon, 244 ends plus 2 floating selvedges = 246 ends, 650 yards (594.4 m)
- Oak, 159 ends, 425 yards (388.6 m)

Weft

Pattern thread: 5/2 perle cotton, Hunter Green, 375 yards (342.9 m)
Tabby: 10/2 perle cotton, Flaxon, 400 yards (365.8 m)

Threading

Border 1: 2 times

Full Motif: 3 times

Partial Motif: 1 time

Border 2: 2 times

Insert appropriate threading for each lettered block.

Incidental threads are indicated in green.

Tie-up

								T	T
8		8		8	8				8
	7		7	7			7	7	
6		6	6			6			6
	5	5			5		5	5	
4	4			4		4			4
3			3		3		3	3	
		2		2		2	2		2
	1		1		1	1		1	

Border 1 — Oak

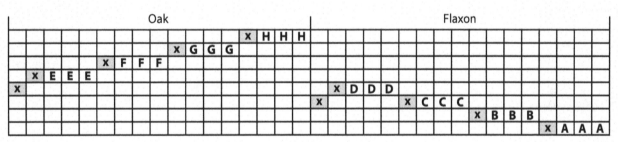

Full Motif — Oak / Flaxon

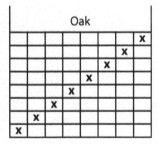

Border 2 — Oak

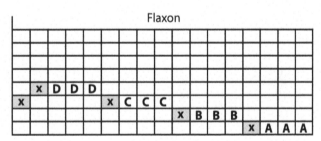

Partial Motif — Flaxon

Treadling

Repeat each treadling 10 times (or as desired).

Repeat full motif to desired length.

Insert tabby between each pattern throw.

Treadling

								T	T
8		8		8	8				8
	7		7	7			7	7	
6		6	6			6			6
	5	5			5		5	5	
4	4			4		4			4
3			3		3		3	3	
		2		2		2	2		2
	1		1		1	1		1	
10									
	10								
		10							
			10						
				10					
					10				
						10			
							10		

Lightning Bolt Scarf

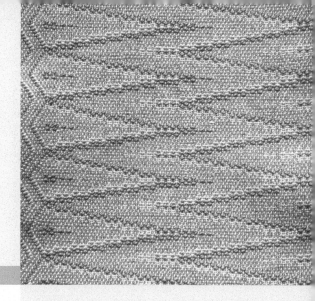

Twill

Treadling crackle weave as a twill opens up so many opportunities for different patterns. I opted to do a relatively simple twill pattern, but if you have a computer design program, you can easily play with the treadling and create your own design. I chose to add a tabby thread after each pattern thread, as doing so opens up the design. For a tighter design, you would omit the tabby thread, creating a more compact design. Begin and end with 0.5 inch (1.3 cm) of plain weave and hem stitching.

I can picture this scarf in so many different colorways. Use a dark background for the warp with a light primary color thread. Another great idea would be to use a gradation of the same color in the warp, keeping the darkest color on the outside and the lightest color in the center. This is a fun method to weave a crackle tie-up. Put on enough for two scarves, treadle them differently, and you would have two completely different creations.

Dimensions: 7.5 x 64 in. (19.1 x 162.6 cm), plus 4-in. (10.2-cm) fringe

Warp

Sett: 24 epi, 12 dent reed, 2 threads per dent
Length: 3-yard (2.7-m) warp
Thread: 10/2 perle cotton, Poplin, 182 ends plus 2 floating selvedge = 184 ends, 575 yards (525.8 m)

Weft

Pattern thread: 5/2 perle cotton, Peacock, 250 yards (228.6 m)
Tabby thread: 10/2 perle cotton, Poplin, 250 yards (228.6 m)

Threading

Border 1: 1 time
Full Motif: 2 times
Border 2: 1 time
Insert appropriate threading for each lettered block.
Incidentals are indicated in green.

								T	T
8		8		8	8				8
	7		7	7			7	7	
6		6	6			6			6
	5	5			5		5	5	
4	4			4		4			4
3			3		3		3	3	
		2		2		2	2		2
	1		1		1	1		1	

Tie-up

						x								x
					x								x	
				x								x		
			x								x			
		x								x				
	x								x					
x								x						
							x							

Border 1

x	H	H																					
			x	G																			
					x	F	F																
								x	E	E													
											x	D	D										
														x	C	C							
																	x	B	B				
																				x	A	A	A

Motif

							x							
						x								x
					x								x	
				x								x		
			x								x			
		x								x				
	x								x					
x								x						

Border 2

								T	T
8		8		8	8				8
	7		7	7			7	7	
6		6	6			6			6
	5	5			5		5	5	
4	4			4		4			4
3			3		3		3	3	
		2		2		2	2		2
	1		1		1	1		1	
X									
	X								
		X							
			X						
				X					
					X				
						X			
							X		
X									
							X		
						X			
					X				
				X					
			X						
		X							
	X								
X									
							X		

Treadling

Treadling

Repeat treadling to desired length.
Add tabby thread after each pattern throw.

Shadows Table Runner

Treadled as Overshot

Lunatic Fringe has a beautiful "Gray Matter" kit that was used to create this wonderful table runner. Wouldn't this be the perfect runner for a modern setting? Just add some lovely pewter tableware and accent with a bright color such as red apples. You could easily change the color palette to fit your home. It would be equally beautiful in shades of green or blue, or how about the Southwest color palette?

Note: This is a 7-harness draft. In order for the transition from Block A to Block G to be correct, an additional incidental thread has to be added. Always remember that you must follow the odd/even rule. I chose to insert the incidental thread before Block A on the number "2" harness. You will see that now when the threading is repeated, you will have two incidental threads together; one will be on harness "2," the other on harness "7." This is perfectly fine, as the threading now follows the odd/even rule.

There are eight repeats of the full treadling motif. Feel free to make this longer or shorter to fit your needs. Begin and end with 0.5 inch (1.27 cm) of plain weave, or, if you prefer, weave 1.5 inches (3.8 cm) of plain weave and finish with a rolled hem. You will notice that the plain weave on one end is Black and the other end is White. It worked out this way because I began with the Black tabby per the pattern and ended with the White tabby per the pattern. You could easily change to make the ends match if you prefer.

Dimensions: 22 x 49 in. (55.9 x 124.5 cm) with 4-in. (10.2-cm) fringe

Warp

Sett: 24 epi, 12 dent reed, 2 threads per dent
Length: 2.5-yard (2.3-m) warp
Threads: Lunatic Fringe "Gray Matter" kit, 10/2 perle cotton, approximately 400 yards (365.8 m) per cone
- Black, 42 ends plus 1 floating selvedge = 43 ends, 120 yards (109.7 m)
- Very Dark Gray, 51 ends, 135 yards (123.4 m)
- Dark Gray, 63 ends, 160 yards (146.3 m)
- Middle Gray, 75 ends, 200 yards (182.9 m)
- Light Gray, 87 ends, 220 yards (201.2 m)
- Very Light Gray, 99 ends, 250 yards (228.6 m)
- White, 111 ends plus 1 floating selvedge = 112 ends, 280 yards (256 m)

Weft

Pattern thread: 5/2 perle cotton, White, 500 yards (457.2 m)
Tabby: 10/2 perle cotton
- Black, 40 yards (36.6 m)
- Very Dark Gray, 40 yards (36.6 m)
- Dark Gray, 50 yards (45.7 m)
- Middle Gray, 70 yards (64 m)
- Light Gray, 75 yards (68.6 m)
- Very Light Gray, 85 yards (77.7 m)
- White, 110 yards (100.6 m)

Threading draft

Light gray	Middle gray	Dark gray	Very dark gray	Black
x E E E E E E				
	x D D D D D			
		x C C C C C		
			x B B B B	x
				x A A A

White	Very light gray
x G G G G G G G	
	x F F F F F F F F

Motif
Repeat 3 times

Threading

Repeat Motif 3 times using the colors indicated at the top of the threading draft. Insert appropriate threading for each lettered block. Incidental threads are indicated in green.

Tie-up

T T

8		8		8	8		8
	7		7	7		7	
6		6	6			6		6
	5	5			5		5
4	4			4		4		4
3			3		3		3
	2		2		2		2
	1		1		1	1	1

Tie-up

Treadling

Repeat each pattern row the number of times indicated.
The pattern thread is 5/2 white.
Tabby colors are indicated.
Follow each pattern thread with a tabby.

Treadling

T T

8		8		8	8		8	
	7		7	7		7		
6		6	6			6		6
	5	5			5		5	
4	4			4		4		4
3			3		3		3	
	2		2		2		2	
	1		1		1	1	1	
6								Black tabby
	8							Very dark gray tabby
		11						Dark gray tabby
			14					Middle gray tabby
				17				Light gray tabby
					19			Very light gray tabby
						21		White tabby

Treadling

Sherbet Towels

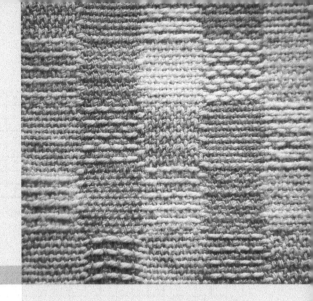

Woven as Summer/Winter

We all can use another set of dish towels, maybe for our own kitchen or as a gift. These would be perfect! If you look at the threading, you will see that the blocks have been mixed around, and the same with the treadling. Study the finished towels, and you still can see a pattern shift across the piece.

I wove this set of towels as one long piece and then cut them apart. This eliminates the tabby weave at the beginning and end, which prevents the towels from puckering at the ends. Just make sure you weave enough yardage for the number of towels you desire.

It would be very easy to change the color combination or to add more colors if you prefer. When weaving, the secondary thread was changed after each block was woven square. This step is optional. You could use the same color secondary thread throughout the piece if you prefer. If you keep the same color, you will lose some of the checkerboard effect.

Dimensions: 14 x 23 in. (35.6 x 58.4 cm)

Warp

Sett: 20 epi, 10 dent reed, 2 threads per dent
Length: 3.5-yard (3.2-m) warp
Threads: 8/2 cotton
- Peach, 169 ends plus 2 floating selvedges = 171 ends, 610 yards (557.8 m)
- Champagne, 170 ends, 610 yards (557.8 m)

Weft

Pattern thread: 8/4 cotton, White, 600 yards (548.6 m)
Secondary thread: 8/2 cotton
- Peach, 300 yards (274.3 m)
- Champagne, 300 yards (274.3 m)

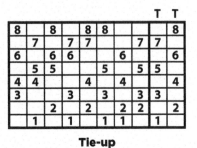

Tie-up

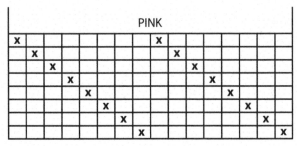

Border 1

Full Motif

PINK | YELLOW | PINK | YELLOW | PINK | YELLOW | PINK | YELLOW

x H H H H
x G G G G
x F F F F
x E E E E
x D D D D
x C C C C
x B B B B
x A A A A

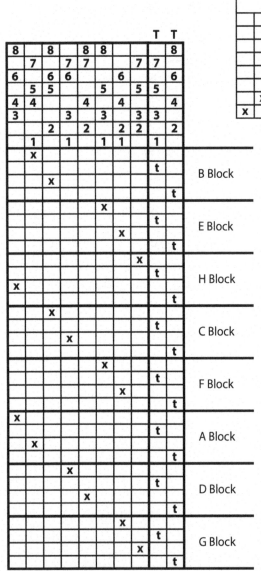

Treadling

B Block
E Block
H Block
C Block
F Block
A Block
D Block
G Block

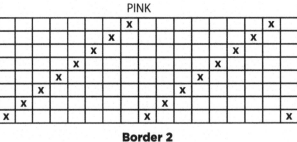

Border 2

Partial Motif

YELLOW

x A A A A

Threading

Border 1: 1 time
Full Motif: 2 times
Partial Motif: 1 time
Border 2: 1 time
Follow the colors indicated at
   top of the threading draft.
Insert appropriate threading
   for each lettered block.

Treadling

Repeat each block to square.
Alternate pink and yellow as
   the tabby colors for each
   block.

Tiny Diamonds Scarf

Classic Crackle

This is a stunning scarf! I used high-quality perle cotton for the warp and secondary thread, which made the tiny 3-thread floats sparkle—like diamonds! The pattern is so very detailed it almost looks like it is a piece of needlepoint.

Notice that I wove this 8-shaft piece with the classic crackle treadling. It works because the blocks are not repeated (with the exception of Block A in the center). As you weave this, you will find that the fell line may start to undulate, but because you quickly change to the next block, the undulation is corrected. And once the piece is off the loom, the threads straighten beautifully.

Begin and end this scarf with 0.5 inch (1.3 cm) of plain weave and hem stitching. The length of the fringe is a personal choice, although I usually have a longer fringe; in this case, I chose 5 inches (12.7 cm).

Dimensions: 9.5 x 62 in. (24.1 x 157.5 cm), 5-in. (12.7-cm) fringe

Warp
Sett: 24 epi, 12 dent reed, 2 threads per dent
Length: 3-yard (2.7-m) warp
Thread: 10/2 perle cotton, Flaxon, 227 ends plus 2 floating selvedges = 229 ends, 700 yards (640.1 m)

Weft
Pattern thread: 8/2 Tencel, Black, 200 yards (182.9 m)
Secondary thread: 10/2 perle cotton, Flaxon, 250 yards (228.6 m)

T **T**

Tie-up

Threading

Full Motif: 3 times
Partial Motif: 1 time
Insert appropriate threading
for each lettered block.

Full Motif

x G
x F
x E
x D
x C
x B
x A A
x H
x G
x F
x E
x D
x C
x B
x H

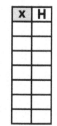

Partial Motif

x H

Treadling

Repeat Full Motif to desired length.
End with Partial Motif.
Insert appropriate threading for
each lettered block.
Incidentals are indicated in green.

A
x
B
x
C
x
D
x
E
x
F
x
G
x
H
x
G
x
F
x
E
x
D
x
C
x
B
x

Full Motif

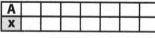

A
x

Partial Motif

RESOURCES

Tom Knisely, Red Stone Glen, York Haven, PA

Weave Classic Crackle: Susan Wilson, Schiffer Publishing, Atglen, PA

A Crackle Weave Companion: Lucy M. Brusic, Kirk House Publishers, Minneapolis, MN

VISUAL INDEX

FOUR-SHAFT PATTERNS

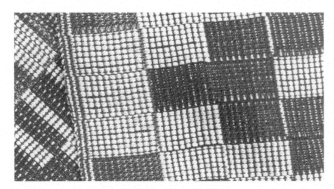

Abstract Scarf **39**

Autumn Table Runner **41**

Baby Blocks Blanket **45**

Blocks of Thyme Shawl **47**

Blue Shadows Scarf **51**

Color Wheel Shawl **53**

Cross Vestment **57**

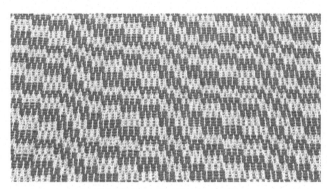

Ebb Tide Table Runner **59**

Gold Leaf Scarf **63**

Gradation Scarves **65**

Hydrangeas Table Runner **69**

Jelly Beans Kitchen Towels **73**

Just for Fun Mobius Scarves **75**

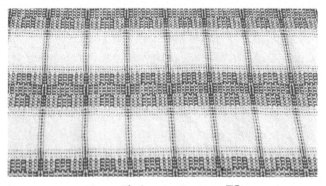

Merry Christmas Runner **79**

Plum Jellies Dish Towels **81**

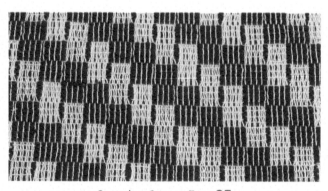

Stepping Stones Rug **85**

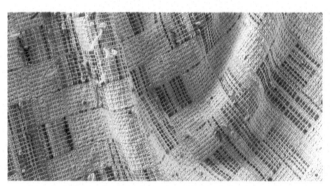

Thrum Throw **87**

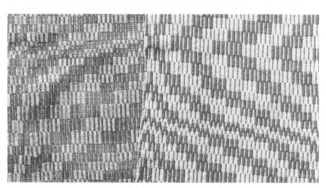

Wavelengths Scarves **91**

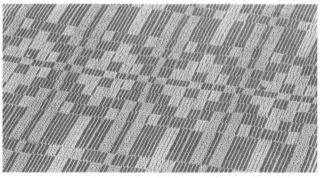

Woodland Path Table Runner **93**

Wrapped in Gingham Scarf **97**

EIGHT-SHAFT PATTERNS

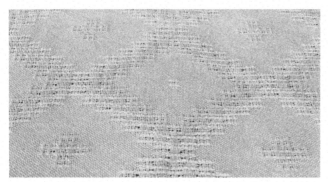

Diamonds and Lace Table Runner **103**

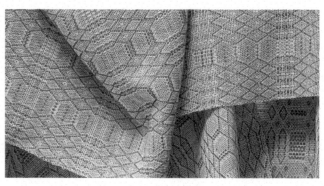

Finale Cape **107**

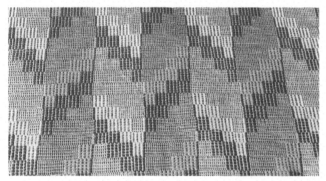

Highlands Table Runner **111**

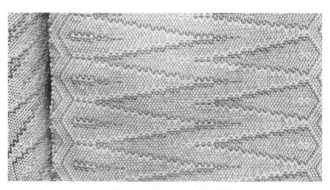

Lightning Bolt Scarf **115**

Shadows Table Runner **117**

Sherbet Towels **121**

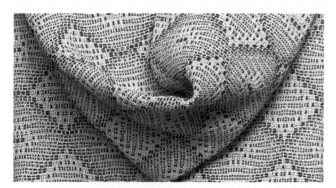

Tiny Diamonds Scarf **123**